The Language of Conversation

'Long awaited by both students and teachers, this book deals with the "nuts and bolts" of discourse in a way that is instantly accessible, and yet has the academic basis required for examination courses.'

Linda Varley, Principal Moderator for Coursework,
A-Level English Language

'This is a wonderful starting point for anyone interested in finding out how the language of conversation works. The issues are clearly related to the reader's own experiences, which makes the subject truly come alive.'

Ishtla Singh, Kings College, London

This accessible satellite textbook in the Routledge INTERTEXT series is unique in offering students hands-on practical experience of textual analysis focused on conversation. Written in a clear, user-friendly style by an experienced teacher, it combines practical activities with texts, followed by commentaries and suggestions for further study. It can be used individually or in conjunction with the series core textbook, *Working with Texts: A core book for language analysis*.

Aimed at A-Level and beginning undergraduate students, *The Language of Conversation*:

- analyses exactly what happens during conversation and why
- discusses the structure, purpose and features of conversation
- explores the relationship between speaker and listener
- examines different kinds of conversation, including television chat shows, door-to-door sales pitch, classroom interaction, teenagers' chat, mother and child communication
- explains the theory in a simple, practical way – without jargon
- provides a clear introduction to technical terms.

Francesca Pridham is Head of English at Winstanley Sixth Form College, Wigan, and Assistant Examiner in A-Level English Language.

The Intertext series

⦿ **Why does the phrase 'spinning a yarn' refer both to using language and making cloth?**

⦿ **What might a piece of literary writing have in common with an advert or a note from the milkman?**

⦿ **What aspects of language are important to understand when analysing texts?**

The Routledge INTERTEXT series aims to develop reader's understanding of how texts work. It does this by showing some of the designs and patterns in the language from which they are made, by placing texts within the context in which they occur, and by exploring relationships between them.

The series consists of a foundation text, *Working with Texts: A core introduction to language analysis*, which looks at language aspects essential for the analysis of texts, and a range of satellite titles. These apply aspects of language to a particular topic area in more detail. They complement the core text and can also be used alone, providing the user has the foundation skills furnished by the core text.

Benefits of using this series:

⦿ **Multi-disciplinary** – provides a foundation for the analysis of texts, supporting students who want to achieve a detailed focus on language.

⦿ **Accessible** – no previous knowledge of language analysis is assumed, just an interest in language use.

⦿ **Student-friendly** – contains activities relating to texts studied, commentaries after activities, highlighted key terms, suggestions for further reading and an index of terms.

⦿ **Interactive** – offers a range of task-based activities both for class use and self study.

⦿ **Tried and tested** – written by a team of respected teachers and practitioners whose ideas and activities have been trialled independently.

The series editors:

Adrian Beard is Head of English at Gosforth High School in Newcastle upon Tyne and a chief examiner for A Level English Literature. He has written and lectured extensively on the subjects of literature and language. His publications include *Texts and Contexts* (Routledge).

Angela Goddard is Senior Lecturer in Language at the Centre for Human Communication, Manchester Metropolitan University and was Chief Moderator for English Language A Level Project Research for the Northern Examination and Assessment Board (NEAB) from 1983 to 1995. She is now Chair of Examiners for A Level English Language. Her publications include *Researching Language* (2nd edn, Heinemann 2000).

Core textbook:

Working with Texts: A core introduction to language analysis (2nd edn, 2001)
Ronald Carter, Angela Goddard, Danuta Reah, Keith Sanger, Maggie Bowring

Satellite titles:

Language and Gender
Angela Goddard and Lesley Meân Patterson

The Language of Advertising: Written texts (2nd edn)
Angela Goddard

The Language of Conversation
Francesca Pridham

The Language of Drama
Keith Sanger

The Language of Fiction
Keith Sanger

The Language of Humour
Alison Ross

The Language of ICT: Information and communication technology
Tim Shortis

The Language of Magazines
Linda McLoughlin

The Language of Newspapers (2nd edn)
Danuta Reah

The Language of Poetry
John McRae

The Language of Politics
Adrian Beard

The Language of Speech and Writing
Sandra Cornbleet and Ronald Carter

The Language of Sport
Adrian Beard

The Language of Television
Jill Marshall and Angela Werndly

Related titles:

The Language of Conversation

• Francesca Pridham

Routledge
Taylor & Francis Group

LONDON AND NEW YORK

First published 2001
by Routledge
2 Park Square, Milton Park,
Abingdon, Oxon, OX14 4RN

Simultaneously published in the USA and
Canada
by Routledge
270 Madison Ave, New York, NY 10016

Reprinted 2002, 2005

*Routledge is an imprint of the Taylor & Francis
Group*

Typeset in Stone Sans/Stone Serif by Keystroke,
Jacaranda Lodge, Wolverhampton
Printed and bound in Great Britain by
TJ International Ltd, Padstow, Cornwall

British Library Cataloguing in Publication Data
A catalogue record for this book is available
from the British Library

*Library of Congress Cataloguing in Publication
Data*

Pridham, Francesca, 1959–
  The language of conversation / Francesca
Pridham.
    p. cm. — (Intertext)
  Includes bibliographical references and
index.
  1. Conversation analysis. I. Title.
  II. Intertext (London, England)
  P95.45 .P75 2001   00–062754
  302.3′46—dc21

ISBN 0–415–22964–2

contents

Contents

acknowledgements

Thank you to everyone who helped me with this book; Ron Carter, Angela Goddard and Adrian Beard for their useful comments on drafts. All the English Language A-level students who have contributed their ideas and in particular the following, whose transcriptions I have used: Sarah Baldwin, Anna Glass, Ben Hart, Andrew Herterich, Gemma Hoare, Philip McNaboe, Natalie Moss, Lee Newton and Vanessa Williams. Friends, and particularly my family, who have allowed me to pursue them relentlessly with a tape recorder. Sue O'Neil for her patience and typing. Steve Waling for use of his poem, 'What She Said'.

The following texts have been reprinted by courtesy of their copyright holders: material from *This Morning* by permission of Granada Television Limited. Material from *Trisha* by permission of Anglia Television Limited.

Looking back over the conversations you've held today, many of them initially seem unimportant and trivial. In fact, some of the conversations we hold are like islands of predictability. In most families, the morning grunting ritual is a 'safe', predictable conversation. So too are those ritual-ised exchanges when you bump into a friend who asks 'How are you?' Almost involuntarily, the predictable response is 'Fine. How are you?'

Some types of conversation are less predictable but also occur frequently. When a friend asks 'Guess what I did at the weekend', and then proceeds to tell us, as a listener, we are involved in storytelling. Many conversations do, in fact, simply involve an exchange of stories as we spend time listening to each other's stories and telling our own.

Conversation often provides people with the opportunity to evaluate and discover themselves. Not all people choose to use conversation in this way to explore personal topics but even in the discussion of impersonal topics such as sport, TV programmes or even the weather, a bonding takes place between speakers who keep the channels of communication open with one another. This can lead to interesting negotiations of ideas and feelings and a conversation can evolve using a structure and language that facilitates this.

In other conversations where we feel the people talking are not of equal status, often the function of the conversation can be different for each of the speakers involved. Parents and teenagers talking to one another can, for example, have different purposes in their conversations, as a parent tries to discover what their teenage son or daughter has been doing and the teenager tries to withhold this information.

Classroom conversation too, for example, is structured in a completely different way from the normal relaxed chat between friends. Both student and teacher, respecting the learning purpose behind talk in the classroom, know the conversational role they should play and structure the con-versation accordingly. It seems that we have, in fact, produced a particular type of conversation to achieve learning in the context of the classroom.

Certain talk situations do tend to be repeated. We are bound, for example, to ask for services at a shop or restaurant more than once in our lifetime. As similar contexts and purposes for talk re-occur, it appears that we have developed a reasonably set method of talking or a conversational genre that covers that particular talk situation. We have created particular **speech events**.

Look at the following examples of spoken language. Decide what type of conversation or genre you feel the example has come from. Explain what language helped you define the nature of the conversation.

1   Guess what I did at the weekend!
2   Thank you very much for listening and if there are any questions, we'll just take them now.
3   I put it to you that, at the time of the accident, you were doing in excess of the speed limit.
4   Good morning. Barnet Leisure Centre. How can we help you?
5   Hello number one, what's your name and where do you come from?
6   Right, we're going on, come on, shush please, we're going on today to look at . . . .
7   How do you do?

Guidelines for taping spoken language

The only way to conduct research on conversation is to tape it, but be sure to follow the guidelines given below.

◎   You need to get permission from speakers before recording them.
◎   Often, at the beginning of the recording, the speakers can be either nervous or very self-conscious. This can make the conversation appear to lack spontaneity. As the speakers warm up, however, they forget the tape recorder is present and relax into more 'normal' conversation.
◎   We can never be entirely sure, however, what is 'normal' conversation. As soon as we attempt to record it, we experience what is known as 'observer's paradox', that is, we cannot be sure how far the observation of a conversation has influenced what has been said.
◎   It would be easier, therefore, at times, to record conversation without people knowing that this was happening. In this situation, ask the person's permission to use the material recorded when the recording is over.
◎   Preserve the anonymity of your speakers and change their names on the transcription.

Text: Joke

right (.) three men sat in a pub (.) and er sat there having a quiet drink (.) and in walks this really drunken old man (.) and he staggers in and he's all over the place he's knocking drinks over (.) he's er standing on people's feet and (.) um all the rest of it and um he walks over to the bar this old man (.) and he orders a pint of lager (.) he er gets his pint (.) and downs it fast as he can in one (.) and then he staggers over to these three men (.) these three men are looking at each other nudging each other (.) right what does he want (.) and ur (.) this man walks over he says (.) I'vehadyermam I'vehadyermam and one of the men says (.) piss off! so (.) this this old man he staggers away and he goes to the bar and he orders another drink (.) another pint of lager and downs this even faster (.) he staggers back over to these three men (.) and he says I've had your mam I've put cream on her body and I've licked it off (.) guy stands up again he says look go away (.) so er this old man staggers back to the bar (.) all over the place he orders another pint (.) this one downs even faster and he comes and again again he comes back over to these three men (.) he says I've had your mam I've put cream on her body I've done things to her you wouldn't understand (.) well they've had enough so (.) one of the men stands up he says look dad you're drunk go home.

Commentary

Your written version will probably have involved several changes. The pauses (.) and voiced pauses (*er* and *um*) disappear. They provide thinking time in the spoken version which is necessary due to the spontaneous nature of spoken language and obviously unnecessary in the planned written version.

The written version will be divided into separate sentences and the heavy use of the co-ordinating conjunction 'and' in the spoken version will have been edited out.

There is frequent repetition in the spoken version. For example, 'this man this man' is repeated twice as the speaker hesitates and takes thinking time to sort out his ideas clearly. The repetition in 'another drink another pint of lager' occurs because the speaker wants to add extra information. The redundancy of this repetition also enables a listener to have the necessary time to understand the joke properly. In a written text, where the reader can refer back to the text and need not understand everything first time through, a writer uses time to plan the text and this repetition will have been edited out as unnecessary.

The words 'right' and 'well', known as **discourse markers** because they indicate the structure of a spoken text, would no longer be necessary in a written text.

Some text will have been added to or modified in the written joke. The phrase 'guy stands up again' – will have been written as 'the guy stands up again'. **Ellipsis** or missing out odd words or phrases often occurs in spoken language where the situation or the speaker himself can make the meaning clear. The word, 'guy' and the expression 'he downs this in one', might have been considered too colloquial and they might have been changed for more formal vocabulary. Depending on the context of the written joke, the taboo language 'piss off!' might also have been considered too challenging for a formal written text, and have been changed for a less taboo phrase.

Any dialect used will have disappeared. The words, 'three men sat in a pub', which open the joke, show ellipsis. This is the compressed form of the regional dialect 'three men were sat in a pub'. In the written version, this would appear in the Standard English past continuous, 'three men were sitting in a pub'.

The **vague language** 'and all the rest of it' would probably have been made more precise in the written version. Throughout the joke 'this' and 'these' have been used – 'this old man', 'these three men'. The original incident took place in the past and the use of 'this' or 'these' brings the characters to life making them more immediate and 'present' rather than distant and past. The words almost imply both speaker and listener can see the men being described. Written language, though, aims for complete clarity and may have rejected 'this' and 'these' as being too imprecise.

In a similar way, the written text would probably have edited out the liveliness and directness of the tense change in the spoken version where the past tense 'sat', at the beginning, changes to the present tense that the rest of the joke is then told in.

The reason for telling a joke is to entertain the audience and the person telling the joke has used spoken language to put on a performance for the listening audience. At times, the speaker has acted out the roles played by the characters in the joke. For example, he has imitated the way he imagines the drunken man would speak, saying 'I'vehadyermam'. These aspects of performance and the prosodic features of intonation, speed, stress and volume are very difficult to capture in a written text.

Text: *This Morning*

> RAJ: and another good answer is I don't know the answer and let's go and
>   find out together
>
> RICHARD: I'll tell you one thing when we moved to London and we'd
>   been here for about a month and we were just driving around looking
>   at the sights and we were driving past Buckingham Palace right and
>   Chloe's in the back of the car right this is so funny um and she said
>   there it is there's Buckingham Palace woah woah oh we should open
>   the window oh and the Queen lives there oh look the flag's up the
>   Queen's in there now and she said is that the Queen's house then? and
>   we said yeah she said ooh fancy building a palace next to the main road
>
> RAJ, R & J: (*laughter*)
>
> JUDY: on the main road (*laughs*) which is logical
>
> RICHARD: which is very observant absolutely why did they do that she
>   said and actually I couldn't think because the road was probably there
>   when they built it although there wouldn't have been cars on it
>
> RAJ: I hope you praised her for making a good point
>
> RICHARD: well we fell apart

Commentary

Richard starts his story with the words 'I'll tell you one thing', a sign that he's going to interrupt the discussion and take a longer turn than usual to tell a story. He starts by giving the background information to the story – the who, what, where and when. The characters are Richard and Judy and their daughter Chloe. The story is set in London near Buckingham Palace after the family has moved there. They're in the car because they're driving round to look at the sights.

The background information is separated from the rest of the story by the two uses of the word 'right'. The main bulk of the story is told in rapid dramatic dialogue, building up to the climax which is Chloe's unanswerable question.

Just before the dialogue, Richard prefaces the story with the words, 'this is so funny', which tells the listeners how he wants them to interpret it. As they all laugh at the end, it is obvious they share and support his evaluation. Richard then explains that he couldn't answer the question that Chloe asked and Raj picks this up, relating back to the previous discussion on children's questions by saying 'I hope you praised her for making a good point'.

14

Richard has a clear reason for telling his story. Just before Richard started to tell the story, Raj had been making the general point that if parents are faced with a question to which they don't know the answer, they should admit this and investigate the answer together. Obviously, this has triggered Richard into remembering a specific story that illustrates how he felt as a parent when faced with a question he couldn't answer. Stories often provide a specific example to illustrate a general point, as a way to make the general point more personalised and understandable.

Judy and Raj have instinctively understood this and have collaborated with Richard at the end to show the relevance of the story – Judy with her appreciation of Chloe's question as 'logical' and Raj by pulling the conversation back to its original topic – parents dealing with children's questions. The story has therefore provided a light-hearted way to learn and reinforce ideas on this topic.

Labov's narrative framework

Richard's story can also be analysed by using Labov's theory of narrative structure (Labov, 1972). According to Labov, in an essay entitled 'The transformation of experience in narrative syntax', narrative is natural to both written and spoken language and its structure can be divided into the following:

◎ abstract (signals that a story is about to begin; is a brief explanation of what the story is about);
◎ orientation (context in which the story takes place, the who, what, where and when of the story);
◎ action (the 'what happened' element of the story);
◎ resolution (what finally happened);
◎ coda (signals end of story and can link back to the present situation);
◎ evaluation (comments, gestures running throughout the story to show how this is interesting).

All these elements are not always present, but this is a useful framework for evaluating oral stories. The elements usually occur in the order given, but evaluation can occur at any point.

Commentary

John first describes how his aunt used to imagine herself being followed. He seems to be critical of this partly because of its effect on his uncle and partly because it was imagined and not real. He then describes his aunt's behaviour at Christmas when she left the room rather then watch him and his brother eat. Again, his final comment, 'we'd eaten three meals a day all our lives and she couldn't watch us eat', appears critical of her behaviour which he implies is illogical and, therefore, strange.

The evaluative comments used about John's aunt are:

◎   they lived in a complete fantasy world;
◎   it's a pure fantasy;
◎   I'll tell you how bad this aunt was;
◎   that is odd actually.

Steve also says about his aunt 'she was so kind of a big character herself'. With John's aunt, the evaluation stresses his aunt's over-active imagination. It's difficult to decide whether 'I'll tell you how bad this aunt was' is simply being negative about the aunt or just stressing how excessive her behaviour was. Steve's final comment, 'that is odd actually', does seem, though, to sum up what the stories have illustrated about John's aunt – that her behaviour was most odd.

Steve, in contrast, does not give a story to illustrate his aunt's character, but John's comment about her husbands, 'they weren't really around were they?', implies he already knows something about her. Steve's comment, however, on how 'big' her character was and his use of the emotive word 'swamped' attempt to portray some feeling of the strength of her personality.

Throughout the conversation, the two men help each other talk about their aunts. John offers a context to place the story in to enable Steve to understand it better when he says 'they had the most wonderful sort of existence because they lived in a complete fantasy world'. He frequently checks Steve's involvement in the story with the **filler** 'you know' which signals the assumption that Steve does understand what he is talking about.

Steve signals the start of his discussion of his aunt when he says 'it's a funny thing'. As a good listener, Steve also laughs in all the right places. He gives constant **speaker support**, continually saying 'yeah yeah' to show his interest and involvement in the story and at the end he joins in with the evaluation of John's aunt, agreeing with what John has said with his utterance 'yeah that is odd actually'.

John first shows interest in Steve's aunt by adding his witty comment about her husbands, 'they weren't really around long, were they?' The negative clause 'they weren't really around long' has had the positive tag question 'were they?' added to it. **Tag questions** are the short two word questions that can appear at the end of a statement or command. Unlike other questions, tags are not always used to gain information, but rather to check out or establish that the speaker and listener share the same mutual view of things. Here, John checks that Steve gets his joke and Steve shows he does by laughing. Later, John takes advantage of Steve's hesitancy and interrupts him to tell another story about his own aunt.

John shows three main ways of bringing his story alive. First, he uses exaggeration and intensification to heighten his story. Look at the following, for example:

◎   the superlative in 'the most wonderful sort of existence';
◎   the repeated intensifier in 'very, very withdrawn';
◎   the adjectives in 'a complete fantasy world', and 'it's a pure fantasy'.

Second, emotive vocabulary is also used:

◎   the colloquial phrase 'feed up his fear';
◎   the verb 'swamped';
◎   the description of his aunt's feelings, 'she couldn't bear to watch'.

Third, repetition also stresses the main points. For example:

◎   'they were sure (.) they were sure that they were waiting outside';
◎   'she couldn't bear to watch us eat', 'she couldn't watch us eat'.

In a variety of ways, therefore, John has made his story vivid and alive.

Summary

People communicate daily through their use of spoken narrative. As in all spoken texts, the features of spoken language that distinguish it from written language will be present. These include: pauses, voiced phrases (*er, um*), fillers (*you know*), repetition, rephrasing, vague language (*sort of, kind of*), colloquial vocabulary, discourse markers (*right, well*), ellipses, context dependent language (*this, these*), frequent use of *and*.

Structure in conversation

We have already looked at the features of spoken language and the storytelling of conversation. Before we look at any other conversational genre, it seems logical to look at the features that can be used by speakers to structure conversation. Because of its spontaneity, there is no conscious plan to build a conversation but speakers with similar knowledge nevertheless work together at structuring and building the various types of conversation that we use daily. This unit looks at the various structuring mechanisms available in conversation.

Sacks, Schegloff and Jefferson (1974) pioneered conversation analysis, an approach to analysis derived from sociology and known as ethnomethodology. It argues that conversation has its own dynamic structure and rules, and looks at the methods used by speakers to structure conversation efficiently. This means they look, for example, at the way people take turns, what turn types there are, such as adjacency pairs and at discourse markers which indicate openings, closures and links between and across utterances.

Two men, Andrew and David, in their early twenties, recorded the following conversation while chatting to each other in David's house. Read the following transcription and answer the questions below:

23

Adjacency pairs

One kind of turn-taking described by the ethnomethodologists is an adjacency pair. This occurs when one speaker's utterance makes a particular kind of response likely. Adjacency pairs are pairs of utterances that usually occur together.

The most often used adjacency pair of the conversation is question–answer. A question, for example, in our culture is followed by an answer and is, therefore, a convenient way to introduce a new topic and to ensure a response.

David uses six questions, each of which gets a response. The level of response varies however, according to the type of question used. An open question usually starts with a 'wh-' question word or the use of 'how' and leaves a fairly open agenda for the speaker answering the question. David's first question, 'how's your dogs', seems, therefore, to be an open, interested and genuine enquiry, but the closed aspect of the question, 'alright', implies that this is a passing reference. David has already assumed the dogs are all right and, really, he is expecting the confirmation he receives rather than a lengthy discussion.

Similarly, David's closed question about the snow – a very safe topic in England – doesn't need much development and though he wants Andrew's support and interaction, his question about little Mr Hudd is really simply to give himself an opportunity to display his own knowledge of Mr Hudd rather than to produce a lengthy response from Andrew. Andrew's answer to 'How's your Mum?', though, is obviously too short for David and he pursues the topic again with another and more precise question, 'Arthritis still bothering her?'

The adjacency pair question–answer helps, therefore, in the structuring of the conversation. How much the question throws open the topic, however, can be dependent on the nature of the question. One of the most interesting types of question that can be used is a 'tag' question. How a tag question operates depends on the intonation used and the context it appears in. A tag question can show tentativeness and can reflect a desire for reassurance, as in 'this is a good match, isn't it?' It can also be a very assertive device in prompting a response and in directing what the response should be, for example, 'You're not leaving, are you?'

In the same way, it is difficult to avoid answering repeated questions and as the urgency of the question increases, the length of the question decreases. In other words, short, sharp questions are forceful in provoking a response.

Look at the following questions and discuss whether they are open or closed? Consider how effective they would be at encouraging speaker participation.

1   Did you enjoy the spaghetti bolognese?
2   Do you love her?
3   I think the Labour candidate's the best, don't you?
4   Are you going to put up with that?
5   What plans have you for the next few years?

Breaking adjacency pairs

As an accepted part of conversational structure, adjacency pairs have strong in-built expectations. Questions are answered, statements acknowledged, complaints are replied to and greetings are exchanged. If the rules are ignored and these patterns are broken, this immediately creates a response.

Look at the following exchanges and discuss how they appear to flout the normal expectations of adjacency pairs. Can you imagine a context that would explain this?

1   A: Hello
     B: Goodbye

2   A: Did you go out with John last night?
     B: Why are you asking?
     A: Why do you think?

3   A: What do you think of this?
     B: Gosh is that the time? I must go!

4   A: Your tea's on the table
     B: (6)
     A: Did you hear what I said?
     B: (4)
     A: Answer me, will you?

The repetition shows the teacher's constant awareness of his larger audience and his purpose – to make sure all his students learn, not just the student he appears to be having a conversation with. Throughout the conversation, therefore, he is at pains by repetition to confirm the class's understanding.

Discourse markers

One word that occurs in the text three times is 'so'. This tiny word, called a discourse marker or **utterance indicator** because it signposts the structure of the conversation for the hearer, is also doing its part to help the audience understand what is being said. On its own, a discourse marker has no meaning. Stubbs (1983) tells us that the function of a discourse marker is 'to relate utterances to each other or to mark a boundary in the discourse'.

Schiffrin (1987) has looked particularly at the way speakers signpost the structure of their conversation through their use of discourse markers and their role in marking the conversation off into sections is clear in the chemistry lesson. Discourse markers are a clear indication that conversation is analysable into units larger than a sentence. Each time it is used, 'so' signposts to the audience that the teacher is closing off his point by summarising it again for them. For example, 'so it speeds up a reaction', reformulates what has just been said, summarising one point before going on to make the next.

The teacher's next point is introduced by the conjunction 'but'. Again, this word, though small, plays a significant role in showing the structure of the conversation. 'But' signals a change in direction from what has just been said and the introduction of new information.

Activity

The following conversation took place between three female teenagers at the home of one of the teenagers. They are all aged 17.
Examine how:

1   the discourse markers 'well' and 'oh' operate;
2   the conjunctions 'and' or 'but' work to signpost the structure of the exchange.

Text: Teenage chat

A: well does Caroline like Jane (.) I don't know to be honest (2) well no
(.) she said (.) she's cold she said (.) she doesn't dislike (.) but they've
never really clicked

K: cold?

A: er yeah

K: Jane's cold?

A: and they've never really clicked (.) but she only has to work for her
three days a week

K: I thought it was erm (.) Irene she didn't like

S: no it's Jane she <u>didn't like</u>

A: <u>oh</u> (.) and she was saying that (.) you know you were saying why
didn't she get any men (.) in the hairdressers (.) she gets loads of offers
she said (.) but they're all from married men (.) who want affairs

Commentary

'Well' appears to have two functions. First, it starts the conversation and
operates as an opener, telling the listener that this is the beginning. It seems
to operate in a slightly different way the second time it appears. A has just
said 'I don't know to be honest'. Two seconds later, she contradicts herself,
saying 'well no (.) she said (.) she's cold'. The 'well' here seems to be used
as a sign that the speaker wants to modify what has gone on before. 'Well'
can be used in a similar way to show a reluctance to give a clear negative
after a closed question. 'Well' can, therefore, signal the opening to a topic
or the modification of a challenging opinion.

'Oh' prepares the hearer for a surprising or just remembered idea and
here, as A interrupts B, it seems also to indicate A's enthusiasm to introduce
the new topic.

'And' is said to be the most common conjunction found in spoken
language. It can be simply the signal for a new idea, joining separate ideas
in a list, as in this conversation. It can also be seen as a marker that joins
the ideas of the conversation together in a temporal sequence with the
meaning 'and then'. The sentence 'he saw his wife and ran away' is not
the same, for example, as saying, 'he ran away and saw his wife'. 'And',
therefore, also seems to be used causally.

'But' in this conversation appears to modify or contradict what has gone on before. In the utterance 'she doesn't dislike (.) but they've never really clicked', though the speaker wants to maintain that Caroline doesn't dislike Jane, the 'but' is a sign that she is going to modify this and contradict it in some way. The second 'but', coming after 'they've never really clicked', is to indicate that, though not really having clicked may sound like they have an incompatible relationship, this is not too difficult to handle because Caroline only has to work for Jane for three days a week.

Other conjunctions, such as 'if' and 'because', which signal cause and effect, can be used to explain the relationship between ideas. Other discourse markers, such as 'right', 'oh', 'you know' and 'anyway' with little meaning in their own right, signal the opening or closure of a conversation or separate out ideas in a conversation. Montgomery (1995) explains that discourse markers 'seem specifically to be designed to move the talk on, to effect transitions between one kind of talk or activity and another'. Between them, therefore, these words work hard to make the participants of a conversation more aware of its structure in a way that shapes and helps their understanding.

Openings, closures and repetition

Like every text, conversations have both a beginning and an end, which is signposted clearly by the speaker. The conversation is created jointly by the speakers, who often use repetition to ensure co-operation and full understanding.

Activity

The following transcription is of a phone conversation that took place when RP, a woman in her early forties, phoned a female school secretary, S, about the opening hours of the school shop. Read the transcription and consider these questions:

1   What marks the opening and closure of the conversation?
2   What role does repetition play in the conversation?

Text: The school shop

S: St Ambrose College

RP: oh hallo (.) um (.) I know it's a bit early in the summer holidays but could you tell me when your your school shop's going to be open?

S: er (2) oh dear (3) second (.) second of August

RP: second of August is that the first time it's open?

S: yeah

RP: right what time would that be till?

S: oh wait a moment 31st August right that (*inaudible*)

RP: 31st <u>August</u>

S: <u>yep</u>

RP: or 31st July?

S: yep sorry I mean 31st July

RP: that's a Monday

S: we're open till 31st July

RP: sorry say it again

S: would be it's closed at the moment until 31st July

RP: right yeah

S: and then it's open ten till five

RP: every day?

S: er Monday Wednesday and Friday

RP: right Monday Wednesday and Friday <u>right</u>

S: <u>yeah</u>

RP: up till term time

S: yep yep

RP: then right that's <u>excellent OK</u>

S: <u>OK then</u>

RP: thank you very much indeed

S: <u>right</u>

RP: <u>bye</u> (.) bye

S: bye

Commentary

It would appear that the secretary has a standard routine for opening a phone conversation when someone rings the school. She simply gives the name of the school. The 'oh' in RP's first utterance possibly reflects RP's surprise at the abruptness of this opening, but is followed by the greeting, 'hello', and then a pause before she goes into her request.

The closure comes when, after quite a confused conversation, both parties are sure that the necessary information has been conveyed. Both parties confirm this by saying, 'OK', and RP marks the end of the transaction by saying 'thank you very much indeed'. The conversation is closed by both parties saying 'bye' to each other.

The closure of a conversation or topic can be signalled in various ways. Probably everyone, for example, has used the line 'I must go now.' A trite cliché such as 'Well, that's life' or the repetition of a phrase can also signal closure.

Openings and closures work like discourse markers in that they signpost the structure of a conversation. They are used in many conversations but where speakers are not face to face, as in telephone conversations, they are particularly obvious, because without body language and a shared physical context, speakers have to signal more clearly what is happening with the words they use. Telephone conversations cannot, for example, simply finish with a silence and because speakers cannot see each other, they have, therefore, to introduce themselves at the start of the conversation more obviously. Openings and closures are therefore more noticeably marked.

Repetition clearly plays a part in the structuring of the conversation. For example, RP repeats '31st August' because it is information she is uncertain about and wants to challenge S to check it. At one point, RP even asks S to repeat what she's said with the phrase 'sorry say it again'. Finally to confirm which days the shop is open, RP highlights the point with the discourse marker 'right'. Repetition has, therefore, played two roles in the conversation. It has enabled the speakers to check and then confirm what has been said. By using repetition, the two speakers have worked co-operatively to ensure that RP has acquired the information she needs.

Structure and context

The people speaking, the relationship between them, the circumstances they are talking in, the subject matter, and their purpose for talking can all influence the structure of a conversation.

Activity

The following conversation took place in the changing rooms before a rugby match as four young male team mates prepare for the game. Read the conversation and answer these questions:

1   What is the purpose of the conversation?
2   Can you describe the structure of the conversation?
3   What is used to signpost the closure of the topic?
4   Collect examples of repetition in the conversation. What effect does the repetition have?
5   What is the relationship between the speakers?

Text: The changing rooms

KK: I've got no socks!

MB: wear them

KK: wear what?

MB: wear them what Bucket give you

KK :   them (.) they're wet and dirty

IW: like your mam

MB: (*laugh*)

IW: that was a good un <u>for me I thought</u>

KK: <u>why what did you say?</u>

IW: you said (.) them socks are wet and dirty (.) and I said (.) like your mam

MB and LN: (*laugh*)

KK: yeah (.) good un Fisher (*referring to IW*) (.) you ugly twat

MB: like your mam (.) it's shit that!

LN: like your fuckin' mam Fisher!

KK and MB: (*laugh*)

MB: the end!

AP: oh (.) I've not <u>cleaned these in ages</u>

MB: <u>that's it</u> (.) don't start with mam jokes!

LN: I will

MB: why?

LN: 'cos I've seen your mam!

ALL 4:   (*laugh*)

(*Team coach enters changing room.*)

CDM: is anybody missing anything?

KK: socks

Commentary

There does not seem to be an obvious purpose to the conversation. The conversation contains jokes, boasting, insults, sarcasm and laughter! Montgomery (1995) talks of a 'ritualised exchange of insults' used by Black Americans and describes 'rounds of insults between players, each successful sound being greeted with laughter or approving comments (e.g. "Oh Lord!", "Oh shit!") in such a way that the exchange typically produces clear winners and losers'. This conversation appears to be an example of ritualised routine male talk with a strong misogynist flavour. Here, the boasting, the repetition of the first joke by IW and the addition of the second joke by LN, almost after the end of the topic, could indicate quite self-conscious banter that verges on competitiveness. MB's insistence on 'the end', and his utterance 'that's it (.) don't start with mam jokes', could perhaps not only be a formal closure for the topic but could also indicate the decision to close the topic down before it got out of hand.

The opening of the conversation is easy to describe. The form of the utterance 'I've got no socks' appears to be a simple statement of fact.

35

Speech act theory explained by Austin (1962) and Searle (1969) doesn't ask what form the utterance takes, but what it does. In other words, it concentrates on the functional intention of an utterance and, in context, the function of 'I've got no socks' would appear to be a complaint. The answer, 'wear them', is, therefore, a helpful way to address that complaint and the first two utterances operate as an adjacency pair: complaint and answer.

Next, an exchange follows. KK initiates the exchange asking the question 'wear what?' The response is clearly MB's 'wear them what Bucket give you', and the feedback starts with KK's 'them (.) they're wet and dirty', and is finished by IW's 'like your mam'. MB's laugh evaluates IW's feedback in the way that shows it was meant as a joke.

Next, we have the clearest form of discourse marker. IW stands back from the conversation and points his joke out to the listeners, giving them his opinion of it by saying 'that was a good un for me I thought'.

KK enthusiastically interrupts to check what he has heard, saying 'why, what did you say?' and another exchange follows. KK's question initiates the exchange, leading IW, in his response, to repeat the whole incident, providing a clear summary of what has been said for his listeners and allowing KK the sarcastic feedback 'yeah (.) good un Fisher' and the insult 'you ugly twat'. MB and LN join in with their own feedback, which ends as KK and MB join in laughter.

We have already discussed the closure of the telephone conversation in the previous transcription. A speaker can also use preclosing signals before the final closure. Here, MB starts with the rather self-conscious preclosure of 'the end'. AP obviously considers the topic closed and hopes to introduce a new one with his utterance 'oh (.) I've not cleaned these for ages,' but as is often the case, if someone introduces a new topic too soon, it is regarded as an interruption and ignored. The last closure appears to be MB's 'that's it (.) don't start with mam jokes', but LN's challenging statement, 'I will', opens up a coda at the end. The final adjacency pair of a question–answer ends the topic with another joke on the same theme, supported by the laughter of them all.

There are many examples of repetition:

MB: wear them
KK: wear what?
MB: wear them

KK: they're wet and dirty
IW: wet and dirty

IW: like your mam
IW: and I said (.) like your mam

MB: like your mam (.) it's shit that
LN: like your fuckin' mam

IW: that was a good un
KK: yeah (.) good un

Here, the repetition seems to go a long way beyond simply being there as a non-fluency feature to gain thinking time. The repetition of 'wet and dirty' comes as IW summarises the main point of his joke. Obviously, the repetition of 'like your mam' operates in the same way to emphasise the joke and builds to a climax, particularly as MB adds the evaluation 'it's shit that' and LN uses the taboo 'fuckin' to put as much stress on the joke as possible. IW could be said to be praising himself with the phrase 'that was a good un', whereas KK is mocking him, as both use the same phrase to mean two different things. In the first exchange, 'wear them', 'wear what?', 'wear them', it seems too as if MB and KK are deliberately repeating and using each other's words. The repetition is a clear marker of a joint production, showing that the speakers endorse each other's utterances. Carter and McCarthy (1997) explain, 'The repetitions across speaking turns are clearly not the work of people responding non-creatively, disinterestedly and automatically; they serve to create a strong sense of rapport and interpersonal involvement.'

The close relationship between the speakers is also shown in the non-standard language that they use. Obviously, the taboo language shows their informality. **Deictics** are words which point to something in the context shared by the speakers, which, therefore, does not have to be referred to by name. This obviously shows the physical closeness of the speakers and often implies the use of body language. That they do not have to explain themselves at length also implies a trust in each other's understanding. In this conversation, the dialect demonstrative pronoun 'them' is used to refer to a pair of socks by both MB and KK.

MB's whole utterance 'wear them what Bucket give you', is also non-standard dialect and the use throughout the passage of 'mam' makes this likely to be a northern dialect that they all share. This places them in the same in-group and the language acts as a reinforcement of the group in the same way as the lexical repetition does.

Grice and the co-operative principle

How did the participants in the conversation recognise the jokes and appreciate the sarcasm? What is it that allows them to ignore the surface meaning and, instead, tap into the underlying meaning? In other words, how did the speakers work out what the utterances implied? Grice (1975), a philosopher of linguistics, accounted for this in his explanation of the co-operative principle. He explained that all participants in a conversation interpreted language on the assumption that the participants in conversation obeyed four maxims:

- be true (the maxim of quality);
- be brief (that is, don't talk too much or too little) (the maxim of quantity);
- be relevant (the maxim of relevance);
- be clear (the maxim of manner).

These are called **Grice's maxims**.

If, therefore, two utterances follow one another, people assume they have some relevance to each other. For example, if someone who says 'I'm tired' receives the reply 'There's the Quality Hotel', the inference is that the second speaker is telling the truth and also knows that this is a relevant remark to make because the hotel is open with beds available to be slept in!

It is obvious that the meaning in a conversation is conveyed, not just through individual words or utterances, but also through the way the utterances interact with one another in a specific context. Because speakers and listeners know they can co-operate in their assumption that the conversation will follow the four maxims, listeners can deduce not only the literal meaning but the **pragmatic meaning** – that is, what the speaker is doing or intending with the words.

Flouting the co-operative principle

Grice has also argued, however, that speakers have two options. They can choose to co-operate in accordance with the co-operative principle or they can choose deliberately to flout it.

As with all rules, if on the other hand a maxim is deliberately broken, for example, the maxim of relevance, this is done to create a certain effect and communicate its own meaning or **conversational implicature**. If someone asks 'When was your first sexual experience?', and receives the reply 'Isn't the weather lovely', the answer's complete lack of relevance shows the speaker's reluctance to pursue the proposed topic. Using Grice's maxim of relevance as a guide, when, in the changing room conversation, therefore, KK refers to the socks and says 'they're wet and dirty', IW's comment, 'like your mam', will cause the listeners to think rapidly. They will automatically want to draw conclusions that show the relevance between the two ideas. How can his mam be wet and dirty like socks? A simple play on words suddenly makes the relevance clear enough for a joke.

Look at the rest of the conversation to see how Grice's maxims are being applied.

Chat rooms

This chapter has discussed the rules we use everyday in our structuring of conversation. One interesting development in these rules has come, however, with the introduction of the Internet and chat rooms.

Chat rooms are where people can meet each other to 'chat' on the Internet. There are public chat rooms where anyone can meet to chat or people can arrange a time to meet people they already know, allowing only the speakers they want into the chat room. The 'speaking' involves typing in a message and waiting for a reply. While waiting for a reply, a speaker can also choose to type in another message to complement the first message or to include a new speaker. This means conversations can be between more than one speaker and that turntaking and topic development can be different from that of spoken conversations. Because the speakers do not share the same physical environment it is easy for them to take on roles, which is why the information a/s/l (age, sex and location) is often asked. It also means that the prosodic features of spoken language are not present. To compensate for this, punctuation and icons such as the smiley face explain the intended tone of voice. Spelling and punctuation conventions are often challenged and the conversations seem to be developing abbreviations, vocabulary and spellings peculiar to chat room conversations.

Two extracts from chat room conversations follow. The first extract is of two people who have previously arranged to talk together for the first time in the chat room. The second extract is of two people who have also met

Summary

Conversation is, therefore, a flexible text negotiated between the various participants in a conversation. The speakers and listeners support and evaluate each other using the known building blocks of adjacency pairs and exchanges and operating with the knowledge of Grice's maxims. Non-fluency features help signpost the structure of the conversation as do openers, discourse markers and closures. This signposting causes the participants to be aware of the conversation's structure, enabling a smooth progression from topic to topic and from speaker to speaker. Finally, the context and underlying purposes of a conversation make its meaning clear to all participants. We are also left to consider whether conversation will develop or change due to the infuence of new technology and the conversations that take place in emails and chat rooms.

Extension

The following telephone conversation took place between two friends: Bhavini, a woman in her late thirties, and Philip, a man in his early forties. Read the transcription and consider how the conversation has been structured.

Text: Bhavini and Philip

BHAVINI: hiya

PHILIP: hiya (2) how are you?

BHAVINI: I'm alright (*laughs*)

PHILIP: you're <u>alright</u>

BHAVINI: <u>just</u> woke up

PHILIP: yeah

BHAVINI: vegged for a bit

PHILIP: right

BHAVINI: it's so funny I got up I had breakfast

PHILIP: yeah

BHAVINI: um (2) probably about half eight or something and then I sat down

PHILIP: <u>yeah</u>

BHAVINI: and then in about five minutes I was off asleep again

PHILIP: (*laughs*)

BHAVINI: just sitting on the <u>settee</u>

PHILIP: <u>yeah yeah</u>

BHAVINI: half awake half asleep. Ian's done exactly the same thing

PHILIP: yeah

BHAVINI: he came back about midnight (1) and I wouldn't say he was drunk but he'd been drinking and er

PHILIP: yeah

BHAVINI: went straight to bed passed out before I even came upstairs

PHILIP: (*laughs*)

BHAVINI: and woke up this morning got up he put the kettle on went down on the settee lay down and was off again

PHILIP: (*laughs*) oh right yes

BHAVINI: it's like the house of the slugs

PHILIP: have you both finished then?

BHAVINI: er not he's got another week to go

PHILIP: he's got another week oh dear oh <u>right</u>

BHAVINI: <u>yeah</u> it's his unpacking week you know well unpacking packing up one school and going to the other school

PHILIP: oh right yeah yeah

BHAVINI: and they have a session or something a bonding session

PHILIP: a bonding session oh that sounds <u>fun</u>

BHAVINI: <u>at the</u> start of the old school start of the new school you have to (1) get together (1) so what are your plans for the day?

PHILIP: erm well I don't really have any I thought I might kind of erm (1) go out and take a walk somewhere actually

BHAVINI: it's very nice and sunny isn't it?

PHILIP: it is yeah that's what I thought actually I'll get out somewhere actually (.) rather than er (.) just going down town or something you know

BHAVINI: yeah

PHILIP: I'll go out and do something (1) so I might erm (1) stick around here till lunchtime get some lunch and then kind of go off Stockport way actually and maybe kind of catch a bus out to er (1) what's that place erm Etherow Park or something like that

BHAVINI: oh yeah (.) right so what I'll say is I'll see you tomorrow at the Quakers (.) shall I?

PHILIP: yeah (.) OK (.) yeah

BHAVINI: then we'll take time for a cup of coffee somewhere (.) alright then so if you're going to go and enjoy yourself today have a nice time

PHILIP: I will do yeah

BHAVINI: and I won't chat now cause I'm going to see you tomorrow anyway aren't I at <u>Quakers</u>

PHILIP: <u>yeah</u> OK

BHAVINI: maybe I'll be late but I'll try not to be

PHILIP: (*laughs*) right

BHAVINI: right I'm going to go now and I'll speak to you again tomorrow then Phil

PHILIP: OK (.) right

BHAVINI: right have a good day then

PHILIP: OK

BHAVINI: OK bye (.) bye then

PHILIP: bye

Activity

The following conversation involves three people. A mother and her daughter Hannah, aged 11, are sitting at home discussing an incident that happened to Hannah. Hannah's friend Sophie, also 11, listens to and appreciates the story. Read the conversation and consider the following questions:

1   Where does first the mother and then Hannah check that Sophie has enough information to understand the story properly?
2   What contribution does Sophie make to the storytelling?
3   Can you find examples where the speakers finish off each other's utterances?
4   What evaluation is given of the story?
5   Where do the mother and daughter disagree about details of the story?
6   To what extent do you feel this conversation shows co-operation between the speakers?

Text: The hernia

HANNAH: well I was pretending to be Popeye walking out of the bathroom with a toothbrush in my hand in my mouth even

MOTHER: I never knew you were pretending to be Popeye

HANNAH: I was I was going phoop phoop (.) Popeye the sailor man phoop phoop (.) and then I slipped on the floor and it just cut the insides of my mouth (.) and you thought it was chewing gum and started pulling on it and I was going aargh

MOTHER: it was this big bubble on her mouth like you know

HANNAH: and it was just

SOPHIE: um

MOTHER: because you know that was the cheek but it was the inside

SOPHIE: like white

MOTHER: yeah and (.) and it just looked like a gobstopper or a big round

SOPHIE: chewing gum

MOTHER: chewing gum thing you know and I said ugh and I sort of tried to

HANNAH: pull it out and she didn't notice I'm going

MOTHER: horrible

HANNAH: oow like that

MOTHER: horrible horrible wasn't it because I I when I realised of course I stopped and said oh no there's something come out of Hannah's cheek

HANNAH: and they didn't (.) they left it for ages and ag (.) no they actually took me to casualty and they said just leave it and it'll clear by itself or something

MOTHER: they had this theory that she could bite it off

SOPHIE: oh that's horrible

HANNAH: yeah no because whenever I bit it by mistake it really hurt but then but then um

MOTHER: she didn't eat

HANNAH: but then my cheek just

MOTHER: you didn't eat did you?

HANNAH: it became a balloon

MOTHER: (laughs) it's a lovely concept that

HANNAH: and Mum still didn't think it did

MOTHER: yes

HANNAH: the casualty said oh yes the casualty said

MOTHER: I did

HANNAH: it would be fine just leave it

MOTHER: I did take you

HANNAH: eventually eventually

MOTHER: take you back

HANNAH: she took me back about two days before we had to go on holiday

SOPHIE: mm

HANNAH: and I waited for my operation and you're not allowed to eat before your operation because in case you're sick and you'll choke on it and they won't know (.) right so she goes so she

she goes here we go just a milk shake and I had about

MOTHER: I was worried about her

HANNAH: an hour left to go

MOTHER: I was worried

HANNAH: about 16 and

MOTHER: I thought she must be hungry by now

HANNAH: she goes have a milkshake and so I drunk the milk shake and just before going to the operating theatre they go (.) has she eaten anything (.) or anything for the last 16 hours like we told you you're not to and so she goes oh well she's had a milk shake and they're like ugh so there I am starving to death for another 16 hours or whatever it was you know

MOTHER: it wasn't that long she's exaggerating

HANNAH: and then um when I finally went to the operation I remember I woke up and you said that I asked for some jam and someth . . .

MOTHER: toast and jam

HANNAH: some jam some um some

MOTHER: sat up and the (.) you were all right in the end see (.) we used to call it Fatty Fred didn't we?

HANNAH: yeah I know (.) why did we call it Fatty Fred?

MOTHER: well I didn't want you to be scared of this horrible fat fat bit in your mouth.

Commentary

Hannah deliberately gives Sophie background information on the nil by mouth policy before operations so Sophie can understand her mother's milkshake mistake the better! After her utterance, 'you're not allowed to eat before your operation because in case you're sick you'd choke on it and they won't know', the discourse marker 'right' signals Hannah's return to the story.

Hannah explains the hernia in her mouth by saying simply, 'you thought it was chewing gum and started pulling on it'. The mother explains further that it was 'this big bubble on her mouth you know', the discourse marker, 'you know', checking out that Sophie does understand what this means and adding too that 'it just looked like a gobstopper'.

Sophie's contribution to this explanation of the hernia is vital. She offers her own description saying it was 'like white'; she gives speaker support, 'um', to show she's listening and then finishes off the mother's description 'big round' with her repetition of Hannah's words 'chewing gum'. (In fact all three speakers repeat the words 'chewing gum' to ensure they have the same picture of the hernia.) Sophie's participation here shows a genuine desire to explore and understand what the hernia looked like. Finishing an utterance for another speaker and repeating their words shows closeness and a real awareness of what they're saying.

In a similar way, the same co-operation is shown when the mother's utterance, 'and I sort of tried to', is finished by Hannah's 'pull it out'. At the end, the same closeness is shown when Hannah's 'I asked for some jam and someth . . .' is completed by the mother's 'toast and jam'.

Mother first evaluates the story as being 'horrible'. Sophie shares this evaluation, agreeing 'oh that's horrible'. The mother also appreciates Hannah's comment 'it became a balloon', by laughing and adding 'it's a lovely concept that'. The mother concludes the story in a positive way, saying 'you were all right in the end see'.

Although the mother's final evaluation sums up both speakers' opinions, there are moments when the two speakers overlap. Hannah, first, ignores her mother's comment 'she didn't eat' and, second, is so preoccupied with the idea of her cheek swelling that she even ignores the tag question her mother directs at her, 'you didn't eat, did you?' When Hannah seems to be critical of the delay before her mother took her back to casualty, there seems to be some overlap of speech as the mother tries to get out her defence, 'I did take you back'. Similarly, overlap occurs as the mother justifies her decision to give her daughter a milkshake, finally saying 'I thought she must be hungry by now'.

There are obviously two speakers telling the same story. At times, their viewpoint differs as the mother thinks her daughter is 'exaggerating' and wants to explain her decision. She does not, however, take over the story from her daughter, but rather complements what she is saying. Though their versions might be slightly different, both speakers seem enthusiastic about telling the story and ensuring that Sophie fully understands the implications of what happened. When they talk at the same time, they simply provide two points of view simultaneously.

On the whole, therefore, the conversation appears co-operative. Sophie works as an active listener. The storytellers build and develop each other's ideas and almost compete to give Sophie the full details of the event. Finishing each other's utterances, using the same vocabulary and offering speaker support and evaluation of the story all show a closeness between the speakers and a positive, active interest in the story itself. Carter and McCarthy (1997) explain that the recounting of personal experience is collaboratively constructed, 'listeners do a lot of work, adding their own evaluations, asking for more details, helping the teller to finish the story'.

Activity

The context for the following transcription is different. It is an extract from a chat show programme where guests come to discuss with the chat show host and the audience their experience of a particular problem. The conversation took place on television and, therefore, although it deals with a personal matter, it is a public conversation. It does not occur spontaneously as the previous conversation did. It has been rehearsed or at least the details fully discussed beforehand. Trisha. the chat show host, has the duty, too, to make sure the story is told in a way that shows the listening public clearly what relevance the specific story has to the general topic under discussion – that people 'can't let go'. The conversation is further complicated by Trisha's need to use the photo props given to the audience to make the story appear more personalised and real. Trisha is obviously aware, too, that there are time limitations on the storytelling. The woman she is talking to, Dorothea, appears to be middle-aged and has been asked to talk about her son's disappearance and the difficulty her husband faces in 'letting go'.

Read the following transcription and examine the techniques Trisha uses to direct the conversation. It might help to compare this with the previous conversation.

Text: *Trisha*

TRISHA: who who in your family can't let go do you think? do <u>you</u>

DOROTHEA: <u>it's</u> my man (.) cannot let go really

TRISHA: Neil

DOROTHEA: Neil yes

TRISHA: who we're going to meet (.) who can't he let go of?

DOROTHEA: of my son (.) my youngest son

TRISHA: tell us tell us about your son we've got a picture of him (*picture appears on screen*)

DOROTHEA: oh he was 28 (.) he used to like to travel a lot (.) he's a handsome young man really good <u>physique</u>

TRISHA: <u>yeah</u>

DOROTHEA: I used to call him my <u>cherub and um</u>

TRISHA: <u>yeah really nice</u> there's a photo of him there he is your cherub (*photo appears on screen*)

DOROTHEA: which on oh yes yes you can see his body

TRISHA: you can see his body as <u>well</u>

DOROTHEA: <u>yes</u>

TRISHA: what happened to him? what happened to him?

DOROTHEA: well he was travelling oh and ah from Australia to New York to go to Marseilles then to go to New Zealand back to New Zealand

TRISHA: so he was part part of a crew of a yacht

DOROTHEA: yes he was then after a few months

TRISHA: yeah

DOROTHEA: we had a couple of police (.) civic clothes policemen to come at the door

TRISHA: ahha

DOROTHEA: and we had our seven-year old grand<u>daughter</u>

TRISHA: <u>yeah</u>

DOROTHEA: with us and they ask us too if we would let her out of the room (.) we thought he was talking about other things the police but then they told us that pirates shot Aran <u>you know</u>

TRISHA: <u>pirates shot</u> your son on the yacht

DOROTHEA: some ahha but straight away I said no no no way

TRISHA: so you don't know what happened really to Aran you just thought the the story about pirates was a bit fishy?

DOROTHEA: oh

TRISHA: but you're grieving differently (.) you said <u>he can't let go</u>

DOROTHEA: <u>very much so</u> very much unable to speak about everything

Commentary

The structure of the conversation is very different. Although this is Dorothea's story, it is Trisha who structures the way it is told, principally through the use of questions which Dorothea answers. Because Trisha already knows the answers, the story almost has the feel of some teacher–student conversations. The initial opening, for example, starts with the question, 'who in your family can't let go do you think?' When Dorothea answers, 'it's my man', Trisha adds the extra information of his name, 'Neil', showing she already knew the answer and is, in fact, elaborating on it.

Trisha also gives Dorothea the direct command 'tell us tell us about your son', handing the story over to her. She also feels able to interrupt Dorothea. For example, Dorothea starts explaining, 'I used to call him my cherub and um'. She pauses and Trisha appears at first to give her speaker support with, 'yeah really nice', but then interrupts her because, at this point, she wants to provide a visual aid for the audience and she introduces his photo with 'there's a photo of him'. When Dorothea begins to give details of her son's travelling and Trisha worries that the audience might not see the relevance of the details, she explains what she thinks the audience needs to know, 'so he was part part of a crew of a yacht' and later she emphasises the main point of the story by repeating, 'pirates shot your son on the yacht'. At the end too, when Trisha wants to relate the story back to the main topic of the programme, she moves quickly away from the discussion of the mystery of Aran's disappearance to its effect on Dorothea's partner with her comment 'but you're grieving differently (.) you said he can't let go'.

This could appear to be an unco-operative conversation in the sense that Dorothea's contribution is structured for her and she does not have the flexibility to explore her ideas in the way she might do in a private conversation.

On the other hand, Trisha is concentrating on ensuring that the audience have heard what they need to hear to understand the story clearly and to be able to relate it to the main topic of the show, 'Letting Go'. Dorothea knows that that is the reason she has come on the programme and the overlap at the end when she rushes to agree with Trisha saying, 'very much so very much unable to speak about everything', shows her eagerness to discuss the main topic. Dorothea also answers all the questions she is set and doesn't avoid any topic or build in silences that might show a reluctance to discuss any of the questions. Trisha also offers Dorothea speaker support and her questions could be seen as a real support to Dorothea to enable her to explain her story clearly and effectively. The role or the status of the speakers can, therefore, influence what methods or techniques they use in conversation, as can the purpose behind the conversation. If Trisha and Dorothea both accept the conventions of this chat show programme, then within these conventions, this is a co-operative conversation.

Politeness

Sometimes, a speaker's role gives them the authority to challenge others as in a teacher–pupil relationship, or as in the conversation between Trisha and Dorothea. Presenting a challenge to someone is difficult. We may want to do something, like offer criticism or refuse to do something, such as comply with a request. Although presenting challenges is difficult, there are ways to present the challenge that are more or less acceptable to the person being challenged. These methods show the need to respect the politeness conventions in our culture.

Brown and Levinson (1978) have studied politeness in widely diverse languages and cultures. They have concluded that, in order to enter into social relationships, all people must acknowledge the face of other people. People have two faces:

Negative face says	'No one has the right to tell me what to do' 'I do not like to be imposed on'
Positive face says	'I have my own value systems that I don't want challenged' 'I want my contributions valued and appreciated.'

You challenge someone's face in two ways: either by telling them what to do, which implies you have rights over them, or by showing you disagree with or do not appreciate their values and beliefs. If you challenge someone's face, they will challenge you back! We use politeness with other people so that they will not attack us.

We have to make a choice and provide a balance between getting a message across directly, which might challenge someone, and getting a message across indirectly, which is more polite but sometimes means the message itself is lost.

Look at the following utterances and decide how they could either challenge someone's face or protect it:

1   If this letter was typed, I'd be very grateful.
2   If it wouldn't be too much trouble, I mean, if you don't mind, I'd be grateful if you'd type this letter.
3   Do you drink tea? – Yes but I prefer coffee.
4   Would you like to come to my house? – Well, I'd love to at another time.
5   Shut the door!
6   I feel really knackered. – Do you? I must admit I am tired too.
7   Could you pass the salt please?
8   Let's go swimming!

The following table shows us how we choose between a variety of expressions which show varying degrees of politeness and face-saving. The straight command, 'Shut the door', does not respect a person's right to have control over their own body. Direct commands like this are only issued by a superior to an inferior. Giving straight commands like this can, therefore, be rude or patronising.

To avoid this rudeness, politeness factors have been introduced into the language, for example:

◎   Please, in 'Shut the door please'.
◎   **Hedges**, such as, 'If it isn't too much trouble . . .'.
◎   Commands hidden as questions, e.g. 'Could you pass the salt please?'
◎   Using provisional language to imply negotiation is possible, e.g. 'if', 'would' and 'can'.

The number of hedges or politeness factors in a request or command is in proportion to the amount that the speaker feels she or he is imposing on the listener. 'If it wouldn't be too much trouble, I mean if you don't mind, I'd be grateful if you'd type this letter', therefore, seems ridiculous because there are too many politeness factors used in relation to the difficulty of the task. Sometimes, to save face, the speaker makes the request as impersonal and indirect as possible, e.g. 'if this letter was typed, I'd be very grateful'.

Table: Politeness techniques

	What was said	How polite is it?
Direct message – threatens face	'Shut the door'	Message clear – challenge to negative face could cause offence
	'Please shut the door'	'Please' indicates awareness of politeness but still could cause a reaction as quite blunt
	'Could you shut the window please?'	Command hidden as question – implies listener has some choice! This saves face.
	'Shall we shut the window please?'	Use of personal pronoun 'we' implies we're in the same in-group, have the same values and are doing the task together. This protects someone's positive face.
Indirect message – no threat to face	'It's cold here'	No challenge here! You can always deny wanting anyone to do anything. Message unclear. Response might easily be 'Is it?' or 'Why don't you shut the window then?'

A speaker can also respect a listener's value system and appreciate it by implying membership of the same in-group as the listener. This can be done by the following means:

◎ using the personal pronouns, 'we' and 'us', e.g. 'let's go swimming';
◎ using the same in-group vocabulary, e.g. using dialect or colloquial language when someone else does;
◎ using **psuedo-agreement** which avoids saying 'no' or disagreeing with a speaker, e.g. 'Would you like to come to my house? – Well, I'd love to at another time.'

Robin Lakoff (1973) has summarised politeness in three maxims:

◎ don't impose;
◎ give options;
◎ make your receiver feel good.

Activity

In the following transcription, an adult education tutor, Simon, is sitting in an adult education classroom with an adult student, James, discussing what pieces of work should be submitted in his final portfolio.

Consider the following questions:

1 At what point in the conversation does the tutor, Simon, offer James criticism of his work?
2 How does Simon attempt to qualify his criticism?
3 How does Simon attempt throughout the conversation to reassure James?
4 Does any one man dominate the conversation?

Text: The portfolio

SIMON: right erm (.) well I (.) there's a lot in these er (.) stories I think they kind of they're the kind of thing that would go well in the (.) in the portfolio erm (.) and I like Canal for instance
JAMES: yeah I've rewritten it <u>erm</u> (.)
SIMON: <u>yeah</u>
JAMES: 'cos I wasn't happy with it I've been trying to write in a more quick style <u>I've</u>
SIMON: <u>yeah</u>
JAMES: been a bit too influenced by reading loads of American people I realise I don't like the style (.) it's over-sentimental and too er detailed (.) and I wanted to get back to a more clipped European <u>style</u>
SIMON: <u>yeah</u>
JAMES: and <u>that</u>
SIMON: <u>yeah</u>
JAMES: so I've sort of reworked it to get it more <u>er</u>
SIMON: <u>oh right yeah</u>
JAMES: I don't want anything that isn't meant to be there I want it to be efficient
SIMON: <u>well</u>
JAMES: (*laughter*)
SIMON: I think that might be good if you wanted to bring in the one that you wanted
JAMES: which I'm pleased with
SIMON: which you're pleased with
JAMES: yeah (.)

SIMON: I don't think there's anything wrong with it <u>particularly. I mean</u> (.) <u>I think</u>
JAMES: <u>but I just think</u>
SIMON: I mean I think well certainly the stories are kind of good enough to go into the <u>portfolio</u>
JAMES: <u>yeah</u>
SIMON: I think (.) I'm trying to remember which one it was there's one where you kind of erm I think it occasionally you're going for something like the idea is you're going to have a clever remark er somewhere <u>in it</u>
JAMES: <u>umm</u>
SIMON: erm erm I think er like that kind of (.) sometimes (.) stops the poetry the the story from being (.) quite as effective
JAMES: you mean that at the end or just anywhere
SIMON: well (.) I think (.) erm (*long pause while tutor looks through stories*) no it's not that one I don't think I think erm I think it's erm (.)
JAMES: are you referring to the end?
SIMON: well not not just the ending no it's it's kind of like the occasional thing that (.) you you're going for a funny remark when it doesn't quite <u>come off</u>
JAMES: <u>right yeah</u>
SIMON: but they actually work as stories

Commentary

Simon's actual criticism of James comes in two places – 'I think er like that kind of (.) sometimes (.) stops the poetry the the story from being (.) quite as effective', and 'well not not just the ending no it's it's kind of like the occasional thing that (.) you you're going for a funny remark when it doesn't quite come off'.

Several elements qualify the criticism:

◎   the vague language such as 'kind of' and 'thing';
◎   the use of 'quite', in 'quite as effective', and 'doesn't quite come off';
◎   the qualification of 'sometimes' and 'occasional'. These clearly modify the criticism and, therefore, make it more acceptable for James.

Throughout the conversation, too, Simon reassures James that, despite his precise criticism of one of the features of James's writing, Simon still thinks the stories are 'the kind of thing that would go well in the (.) in the portfolio'. Later, he also says, 'I think well certainly the stories are kind of good enough to go into the portfolio', and finally he ends the conversation with 'but they actually work as stories'.

It is difficult at first to see who leads the conversation. Both men appear to speak for roughly the same amount of time. Though Simon starts the conversation, he allows James to explain and explore how his ideas about writing have developed and offers him speaker support, 'yeah' and 'oh right yeah', to encourage him to explain himself. On the other hand, Simon does still stick to his agenda. James announces that 'I don't think there's anything wrong with it particularly', but despite his confidence, Simon interrupts and pursues his point to come eventually to his criticism. Simon's hesitancy is also interesting. He repeatedly pauses and uses voiced pauses, 'er' and 'um', to give himself thinking time. These hesitations also operate to make the criticism less of a clear challenge. By the end of the conversation, James, when he asks the question 'are you referring to the end?', is even asking Simon to clarify the criticism which seems to imply his acceptance of it.

This desire to be careful in giving criticism reflects Simon's awareness of the importance of politeness and the need for face-saving techniques when giving criticism.

Unco-operative conversation

Sometimes, participants in a conversation, however, simply do not want to co-operate. As there are techniques for co-operating, so, too, there are methods to avoid politeness or negotiation!

The following conversation is between a mother and son, Matthew. The son, playing happily on his computer, is resisting his mother's attempts to persuade him into other activities. Read the transcription and discuss:

1   What methods does the mother use in her attempt to persuade her son to action?
2   What methods does Matthew use to resist his mother?

Text: Matt's resistance

MUM: Matt what are you doing? (1)

MATT: the computer

MUM: could you turn the music down then please (1) (*music turned down*) thanks (1) Matt (1) what do you want to make me a cup of coffee (2)

MATT: in a minute (1)

MUM: in a minute when Matt? (5) it's been a minute now

MATT: (*sighs*)

MUM: pardon?

MATT: no (1)

MUM: are you going to do your bedroom?

MATT: no (2)

MUM: Matt you could do your bedroom couldn't you because you're halfway through (.) you nearly fini<u>shed</u>

MATT: <u>later</u>

MUM: later when Matt? (2) what?

MATT: go away

MUM: go away! (4) Matt you could do your bedroom or you could go into Audenshaw and get your glasses which you going to do?

MATT: I'll get my glasses later

MUM: what about the bedroom? (2)

MATT: I'll do that in a bit

MUM: please Matt (4) what about that cup of tea now then cup of coffee (1)

MATT: no (*almost inaudible*)

MUM: what? (1) you just said no!

MATT: (*inaudible*) care

MUM: what?

MATT: I don't care

The mother attempts to interact with her son by using a series of mainly closed questions working on the assumption that a question has to be answered. The first question, although an open one, asks the obvious and, therefore, probably functions more as an opener.

Interestingly, throughout the conversation, the mother uses a series of politeness features in an attempt to negotiate with Matthew. The commands are presented as questions, 'could you turn the music down then?', 'please' and 'thanks' are both used. The provisional, 'could', implies that Matthew has a choice. At one point, the mother builds in a choice between two options, 'you could do your bedroom or you could go into Audenshaw and get your glasses which you going to do?' At this point, where she gives the limited choice of two options, she receives the conversation's most positive sounding response, 'I'll get my glasses', though the addition of the word 'later' makes it still ambiguous whether he will actually go or not. Robin Lakoff (1973) maintains that the essence of politeness is (a) not to impose; and (b) to give options. The mother appears to be doing both these things, using as many politeness factors as possible to obtain a response from her son.

She also uses the tactic of repeating and building on Matthew's utterances in a way that previously we have seen in co-operative conversation. For example, 'in a minute' from Matthew is followed by 'in a minute when Matt?' and 'later' from Matthew is again followed by 'later when Matt?' It's obvious though, in these two cases, the repetition rephrased as a question certainly keeps the conversation on topic but since these are topics Matthew has tried to avoid, the technique serves not to reinforce what Matthew has said but to challenge it.

The constant repetition of her son's name, 'Matt', when she addresses him, also seems to indicate someone continually attempting to gain the listener's attention.

Despite the fact that Matthew does not appear to want to do anything, neither does he appear at first to want to challenge his mother openly. He responds to his mother, first with his reply 'the computer' and, second, simply by turning the music down.

At the beginning, he avoids answering 'no' to her request 'do you want to make me a cup of coffee?' though his 'in a minute' is more of a psuedo-agreement than a real desire to comply with her request. The direct question 'are you going to do your bedroom?' gets the challenging response 'no', with no explanation or excuse given. In these responses, Matthew, therefore, shows the use of two policies. He knows the politeness strategy of a psuedo-agreement that saves his mother's face, but doesn't actually commit him to action. He can also give a direct confrontational 'no' which challenges face in a way that could cause his mother to retaliate.

He also shows, even more directly, unco-operative behaviour in a direct challenge to his mother's negative face when he gives her the command, 'go away'. Later, too, he challenges her positive face and value system when he says, 'I don't care', and clearly rejects her agenda.

Less obviously though, he has already shown his rejection of her agenda. His responses have broken Grice's maxim on length of utterance. Usually summarised as be brief, it, in fact, requires a speaker to give a response of the right length – neither too long which becomes a performance, nor too short which indicates a lack of interest in the topic under discussion. Matthew's answers are generally too short, particularly where he refuses to give the customary excuse or explanation which should come after a negative response to a closed question.

His use of silence, too, is a strong weapon. One question, 'in a minute when Matt?', gets no response at all, which shows a complete abdication of interest and involvement. At other times, even though he does give a minimal response, the time it takes him to respond is longer than normal, showing his reluctance to talk. One response is just a sigh. The only time he answers at speed is when he almost interrupts his mother's remark 'you nearly finished' with his snapped out 'later'.

This, therefore, is an example of a conversation where the mother uses politeness features as a negotiating tool to attempt to interact with her son. In response, he uses some politeness features to avoid open confrontation, but also uses clear techniques to be as unco-operative as he can without having an open argument.

Activity

There are more obvious ways of being confrontational and unco-operative. Again, this is a conversation between a teenager, this time a daughter and her mother. It is obviously an open argument. Read the transcription and attempt the following questions:

1   What topic is Ruksana trying to avoid discussing?
2   What techniques does she use to be unco-operative?
3   How does her mother try to keep Ruksana on the topic?

Text: The argument

MUM: I just want a bit of appreciation for try (.) the effort I made on your birthday (.) I was almost dying on your birthday (1) don't you realise how much effort it was for me to go there? (1)

RUKSANA: oh sorry make me feel guilty about my birthday 'cos that's so good isn't it?

MUM: make you what?

RUKSANA: do you make me feel guilty about going out on my birthday

MUM: no you should

RUKSANA: shut up

MUM: no you should feel guilty about not

RUKSANA: no you should feel guilty

MUM: about what?

RUKSANA: about holding your illness over going out on my birthday

MUM: I haven't held it against you I just

RUKSANA: well you just did then

MUM: why? (1) I held your ungratefulness against you

RUKSANA: I think you should stop this now

MUM: I'm showing you how illogical your argument was

RUKSANA: how illogical my argument was (.) you sat there saying to me that it's my fault that you were ill on my birthday

MUM: no

RUKSANA: your fault you dragged yourself out

MUM: no I didn't say that I said that you were ungrateful

RUKSANA: I mean it's like an effort that you dragged yourself out for my birthday well I'm sorry

MUM: well it was an effort

RUKSANA: for having my birthday

MUM: I did drag myself out (.) I showed how much I loved you did you show how much you loved me by being sensitive? I've

RUKSANA: oh shut up

Commentary

Ruksana's mother obviously wants to discuss what the mother sees as her daughter's ungratefulness and introduces the topic with the rhetorical question, 'don't you realise how much effort it was for me to go there?'

First, instead of responding to her mother's topic after a second's pause, she introduces her own topic. She says her mother wants her to feel guilty about having a birthday. Ruksana's use of 'oh sorry' would normally be a polite, co-operative way of dealing with her mother's complaint, but she uses it sarcastically, which implies a challenge to her mother and a rejection of her mother's complaint.

Ruksana also attempts to close down the conversation, rejecting it completely at times, with the straight command that she uses twice, 'shut up'.

She also interrupts before her mother can finish the explanation of her point. When, for example, her mother says 'no you should feel guilty about not . . .', Ruksana rejects the complaint with her own attack, 'no you should feel guilty'. Instead of answering her mother's complaint, therefore, Ruksana challenges her mother with the idea that she should feel guilty.

Her exaggeration and emotive use of the word 'dragged' try to imply even more that her mother is guilty of emotional blackmail. One of Ruksana's strongest techniques is to state as a fact something that is blatantly not true when she says, 'you sat there saying that it's my fault that you were ill on my birthday'.

Ruksana's tactics are very unco-operative. The two speakers are not negotiating the topic. Before the mother can get Ruksana to answer her complaint about Ruksana's ungratefulness, she has to deal with Ruksana's accusations. Ruksana's attack means the mother is, at one point, left defending herself and denying Ruksana's charge with 'I haven't held it against you'. She has to state clearly that she hasn't blamed Ruksana for her illness saying, 'no I didn't say that', and to attempt to get Ruksana to answer her original complaint, she keeps repeating 'I held your ungratefulness against you', and 'I said that you were ungrateful'. The mother also shows some understanding of Ruksana's technique by saying, 'I'm showing you how illogical your argument was'. At the end, though, the mother's final question, 'did you show how much you loved me by being sensitive?', still remains unanswered.

In this conversation, there are few pauses. Both participants speak rapidly and interrupt to correct and criticise each other, their simultaneous talking showing a lack of co-operation. Each fights for her own agenda and neither really takes on the other's complaint or answers it adequately – a technique that politicians are often accused of using.

Summary

In order to consider properly whether someone is being co-operative or not, it is necessary to consider the role and status of the speakers. A teacher who directs a lesson, for example, is not necessarily being aggressive or unco-operative with students because he or she chooses to lead them – that is part and parcel of the job. It is not easy to state unequivocally that any one technique is always used, either unco-operatively or co-operatively. Politeness techniques used persistently can, for example, be almost as intrusive as more aggressive techniques; it depends on what purpose they are used for. The context of the conversation needs to be considered carefully in analysing who is co-operative or unco-operative.

Features that could be useful to examine when considering politeness include the following:

open questions	pauses	please/thanks
closed questions	voiced pauses	hedges
tag questions	refusal to take up topic	provisional language
questions with built in options	Grice's maxims	vague language
commands	repetition	inclusive pronouns 'we' and 'us'
interruptions	discourse markers	speaker support
overlaps	finishing utterances for others	use of similar vocabulary

Extension

1   There has been much discussion about the different conversational styles of men and women. The argument used to be that women lost power with their 'tentative' style of negotiated conversation and men gained power with their aggressive style. This is now seriously challenged and instead the different strengths of the two styles are emphasised (see *Language and Gender*, Goddard and Patterson, 2000). Record and transcribe two separate groups negotiating a task – one female group, one male group. Compare their conversational style.

2   Politicians are often accused of being unco-operative, particularly when interviewed in public. This is a charge they would deny. Watch a TV programme such as *Question Time*, where politicians not only have to give their opinions, but also have to compete or negotiate for their turn to impress the listening public. Transcribe a section of the programme and analyse it for features of co-operative and unco-operative language behaviour. See *The Language of Politics*, Beard (2000).

Conversational genres

Aims of this unit

Cook (1989) explains that schemata 'are data structures representing stereotypical patterns which we retrieve from memory and employ in our understanding of discourse'. This means that as speakers, we take some mutually shared knowledge for granted. For example, we assume a shared knowledge of how the world works and interpret what is said by referring to this knowledge. This also explains why we construct varied conversational genres.

Goffman (1974) and Gumperz (1982), were exponents of **frame theory**. This theory argues that we use past experience to structure present usage. As we talk, we pick up cues (or frames) which enable us to recognise the situation and we structure our responses appropriately. These frameworks help us to interpret the conversation and anticipate what is going to happen next. In this way, 'asking for goods' or 'attending a job interview' have particular frames leading to a particular discourse structure or conversational genre.

According to the context and purpose of conversation, different features of conversation are exploited. As similar conversations occur, it appears that in the same way as we have developed storytelling, we have developed other conversational genres. It is argued that each genre appears to have a unique structural pattern of its own. This unit, therefore, explores features of some of the possible conversational genres.

Comment and elaboration

This is one of the most common genres of conversation, usually found in informal conversation, between speakers who know each other well.

Its most common features are:

◎   Topics switch freely.
◎   Topics are often provoked by what speakers are doing, by objects in their presence or by some association with what has just been said.
◎   There does not appear to be a clearly defined purpose for the conversation.
◎   All speakers can introduce topics and no one speaker appears to control the conversation.
◎   Speakers comment on each other's statements.
◎   Topics are only elaborated on briefly, after follow-up questions or comments from listeners.
◎   Comments in response to a topic often include some evaluation.
◎   Responses can be very short.
◎   Ellipsis is common.
◎   The speakers' co-operation is often shown through speaker support and repetition of each other's vocabulary.
◎   Vocabulary typical of informal conversation will be present, such as clichés, vague language and taboo language.

Activity

The following conversation took place on a car journey between two sisters. Kathy is 41 and a teacher. Julie is 49 and runs her own soft furnishing business from home. They are driving to the local town where they intend to go shopping together. Kathy has recently had a minor operation and is at home on sick leave. Their mother lives some distance away. Read the transcription and discuss how far it uses features of a comment and elaboration genre.

Text: Two sisters

KATHY: I had a cup of coffee in the Thornton's shop 'cos I thought I'd give myself come <u>caffeine</u>

JULIE: <u>good idea</u>

KATHY: to keep going and then I just struggled back home and lay down on the settee didn't have lunch was just so knackered by going to <u>Stafford</u>

JULIE: <u>oh dear</u>

KATHY: isn't that weird?

JULIE: yeah (.) are you hungry now?

KATHY: oh yeah

JULIE: I got on the scales this morning I've put a load of weight on

KATHY: oh shit

JULIE: I mean half way back to what I was before

KATHY: oh no Julie that's not on is it?

JULIE: so I've just got my <u>new season ticket</u>

KATHY: <u>you were so good</u>

JULIE: to go swimming

KATHY: yeah

JULIE: and I'm just gonna have to do it all again

KATHY: yeah

JULIE: it seems a shame doesn't it <u>to do it twice</u>

KATHY: <u>I've got to do</u> it as well (.) I was really worried in that hospital looking at all the people there thinking God (2) if you go in Sainsbury's do you have to pay?

JULIE: well you don't have to pay but you have to buy something from Sainsbury's and (1) then you have I think it's an hour or two hours (1) we'll um we'll just stop here

KATHY: yeah have a look round first

JULIE: well we're going up tomorrow to see Mum um

KATHY: yeah are you going all day tomorrow then?

JULIE: she wants me to dream up something to have for lunch (.) should do a pudding but I don't know what to do (1)

KATHY: well get yeah (.) get some winter fruits (.) and make um (.) summer pudding you get the idea frozen <u>winter fruits</u>

JULIE: <u>yeah</u>

KATHY: you do put them in bread don't you 'cos Mum likes <u>summer pudding</u>

JULIE: <u>yeah</u> (*inaudible*)

KATHY: that's right you can have um (1) yoghurt with that can't you as well or (.) instead of ice cream or cream can't you?

JULIE: that all right that is

Language in action

Language in action is defined as language used when people are doing something. The language, therefore, accompanies the task in hand.

Activity

Again, the following transcription is between two female friends in their early forties. Read the text and answer the following questions:

1   At what point in the conversation do you realise what's happening?
2   Why is it difficult sometimes to ascertain exactly what the speakers are discussing?
3   Why are there long silences?
4   Look at the questions in the transcription. What purpose do they serve?
5   What features of informal co-operative conversation can you find?

Text: Parking problems

FIONA: there you are there's a is that a space?

JEAN: oh God it's a bit <u>tight</u>

FIONA: I wouldn't get in that <u>one</u>

JEAN: I don't know

FIONA: what about this one? can you get in that one? (2)

JEAN: that's alright (.) now what's the parking here?

FIONA: oh I don't <u>know</u>

JEAN: <u>half an</u> hour

FIONA: oh that's no good then is it? (2)

JEAN: where is the shop anyway?

FIONA: just keep going down the <u>left</u> <u>there's a</u>

JEAN: <u>going</u> down is it?

FIONA: (*inaudible*) yeah (2)

JEAN: right (1) let's just keep

FIONA: going under this shop here (3) oh where is it now? (.) yeah I went <u>out here</u> <u>um</u>

JEAN: <u>I'll</u> park right

FIONA: oh (.) right

JEAN: oh this one on the left here

FIONA: this one? (.) it looks alright doesn't it?

JEAN: oh there's enough room here

FIONA: do they not want you here because of the loading stuff?

JEAN: <u>no those</u>

FIONA: <u>what are?</u>

JEAN: those aren't in use are they? (2) is that it over <u>there?</u>

FIONA: <u>the</u> Greenhouse yes (4) oh it says drop in for afternoon tea (*laughs*) if we stay long enough we can go to the afternoon tea (4) oh you're good at doing this

JEAN: am I?

FIONA: much better than me anyway (4) do you think it means over there is a car park? (3)

JEAN: got loads of room anyway (*inaudible*) and we've got half an hour to eat

FIONA: that should be alright shouldn't it?

JEAN: whoops that's very handy isn't it? (2)

FIONA: OK

Commentary

It becomes clearer as the conversation develops that this is actually a transcription of two people in a car talking while the driver parks. There is no introduction to the topic, but probably, by the time the reader gets to the question 'Now what's the parking here?', they are aware that this is what is happening.

The conversation is very dependent on the immediate situation. Because both speakers can see exactly what is going on, it would be redundant and unnecessary to describe things right in front of them or actions that are taking place. This means there is much deictic reference with the use of words such as 'that', 'this', 'here' and 'there', 'this one' and 'that one', all pointing to what can obviously be seen by both speakers. There is also much ellipsis. According to Carter and McCarthy (1997), 'Ellipsis is a linguistic concomitant of informality and easy-goingness in conversation.' Here, both speakers know each other well. They share the mutual knowledge of the same situation and are participating in the same activity. Because of their relationship and mutual knowledge, the speakers can take much for granted and they do not need to elaborate and explain themselves fully. Indeed, if they did, they would sound formal and long-winded. Jean can, therefore, say 'I don't know', instead of 'I don't know if I can get in', or later can say 'got loads of room' instead of 'I've got loads of room'. They also share the same assumptions and in, for example, Fiona's utterance 'do they not want you here because of the loading stuff?' the vague 'they' could be understood by both speakers to mean some unnamed agency with the authority to dictate where parking was or was not allowed. All these are features of language in action.

Silence can appear in conversation as a breakdown in communication. Here, both speakers would be unchallenged by the silences because they occur while the speaker is concentrating on an activity. For example, while a driving manoeuvre is taking place, both speakers will be silent to allow the driver to concentrate better. Again, these silences are a common feature of language in action.

There are many questions in this transcription. Some questions are obviously simply there to check information, for example, when Jean says 'where is the shop anyway?' and 'is that it over there?' Some questions seem deliberately used to build in a tentativeness. At the beginning of the conversation, Fiona starts, for example, with a statement, 'there's a', but self-corrects to turn what she is saying into a question, 'is that a space?', instead of making a statement that could be challenged. This tentativeness is a powerful tool to facilitate the conversation. It stops the speaker sounding inappropriately assertive and allows the listener the chance to negotiate and explain their point of view. Coates (1986) argues that 'Questions are powerful linguistic forms; they give the speaker the power to elicit a response from the other participant(s).' They are 'exploited by women speakers who use questions and tag questions to keep conversation going'. Tag questions also seem an important feature in this conversation. The end of the conversation, for example, shows both speakers using tag questions:

> F: that should be alright shouldn't it?
>
> J: whoops that's very handy isn't it?

Neither speaker attempts to reply to the other's tag question or seems to expect a reply. The questions appear to reinforce the intimacy and closeness of the speakers as they seem to signal an assumption of the listener's agreement.

Some of the vocabulary used would only be found in an informal context. 'Just', the phrase 'oh right' (an informal answer showing a clear understanding of the previous utterance) and the expression 'loads of room' are all examples of informal vocabulary. The vague language of 'loading stuff' again is indicative of informal conversation. Many other features show the informality of the conversation. The speakers are comfortable enough with each other for many overlaps to occur. Some questions remain unanswered, for example, Fiona's 'what are?' and also 'oh where is it now?' Fiona introduces a topic with the unfinished utterance 'yeah I went out here um', and the speakers are familiar enough with each other for these breaks in the normal patterns of conversational behaviour not to matter. They finish off each other's utterances, for example, Jean's 'let's just keep' is finished by Fiona's 'going under this shop here', and, with the already discussed use of ellipsis and tag questions, the speakers show a mutual understanding and tolerance of each other.

Summary

◎ People using language in action frequently do not mention what is directly in front of them. They have no need to because they share the same context.

◎ They refer to what they can see with words such as 'that', 'there', 'it' and 'here'. This is called deictic reference.

◎ There can be much ellipsis.

◎ There can be more silence than normal while activities take place.

Service encounters

A **service encounter** is the term used to describe a wide range of conversations whose principal purpose is transactional. These, therefore, are conversations where people want to get things done.

Activity

Read the following transcription. Decide what is happening here.

Text: Eating out

ELIZABETH: um is that coleslaw in the middle there?

ASSISTANT: it is yes

ELIZABETH: I'll have that then please (1)

JENNY: I'll have a bread roll please (.) got to have bread haven't I?

ELIZABETH: (*laughs*) (2) that's lovely thank you

. . .

ELIZABETH: can I have a cup of coffee as well?

ASSISTANT: with milk?

ELIZABETH: please yes (3) I do (.) I do like scones (.) it's my treat on Friday to have a scone (3) thank you (.) we'll come back for pudding shall we?

JENNY: yeah

Commentary

This is obviously a transaction that's taking place in a café or restaurant of some sort. In fact, the conversation takes place between two women in their thirties, going to lunch together. Brown and Yule (1983) have described conversation as being either transactional – language used to exchange goods or services – or interactional – language used for socialising – and the language in this conversation is obviously used for transactional purposes. In this case, that means the language is used to ensure that the customers, Elizabeth and Jenny, get the food and drink they want from the assistant. This kind of transaction, where requests for service are made by one person to another, has been called a service encounter. Eija Ventola (1987) identified the elements that are obligatory in a service encounter as being:

69

◎   an offer of service;
◎   a request for service;
◎   a transaction;
◎   a salutation.

Can you find these elements in the above transcription? They are fairly easy to find. The assistant confirms coleslaw is on offer. She is then asked for it, 'I'll have that then please', and a transaction takes place. The end of the transaction is marked by the words 'thank you', in the phrase 'that's lovely thank you'. Although this is transactional language, the speakers still use the politeness features of 'please' and 'thank you' to interact and to show respect for the individuals concerned in the transaction. At the end of the conversation, too, Elizabeth's final utterance shows an interesting mixture of language. Even while a transaction is taking place, Elizabeth uses language in an interactional way to pass on personal information when she says 'I do (.) I do like scones (.) it's my treat on a Friday to have a scone'.

Activity

The following transcription is of a conversation that took place between a housewife in her forties and a door-to-door salesman, probably in his early twenties. The salesman has called at the door with a bag full of household goods, such as dusters and dishcloths. He is displaying the goods to the housewife in an attempt to sell them to her. She is investigating what he has to offer before agreeing to purchase something. Read the transcription and answer the following questions:

1   What questions does the housewife ask and why?
2   What examples of ellipsis and context-dependent language can you find? Why are they present?
3   How are discourse markers used here?
4   What signals the completion of the transaction?
5   What features of dialect can you find?

Text: The door-to-door salesman

SALESMAN: anyway, there's yellow dusters er dishcloths um oven gloves is like them ones and them ones er there's demist pads (.) there's gentlemen's socks er Ken Dodd tickle sticks um

HOUSEWIFE: it's a weird assortment of things in't it?

SALESMAN: yeah there's hankies (.) well there's men's and then there's ladies' hankies as well right we got super scissors you can use these for flowers for cutting food and they've got like a wire stripper on as well

HOUSEWIFE: yeah

SALESMAN: um (4) then (.) also (.) this is like (.) got all sorts of different bits in (.) if you have an accident

HOUSEWIFE: yeah

SALESMAN: but (.) uh (.) it's not very optimistic is it if (.) I mean I suppose it's always there if you need them (.) uh (.) anyway there's chamois leathers like different types sponge mitts

HOUSEWIFE: it's a what?

SALESMAN: sponge mitts that goes on your hands for washing stuff and then super chamois (.) uh (.) them are reduced from marked price them ones

HOUSEWIFE: how much are they then?

SALESMAN: uh supposed to be eight ninety nine but they're two quid off (.) you can put them in washer

HOUSEWIFE: they'll still be six ninety nine wouldn't they?

SALESMAN: yeah

HOUSEWIFE: yeah okay (*inaudible*)

SALESMAN: um (.) and then we got dishcloths (.) floor <u>and</u>

HOUSEWIFE: <u>how</u> much is the sponge mitts?

SALESMAN: ah three ninety-nine

HOUSEWIFE: they're not very cheap then are they?

SALESMAN: I don't know love cos <u>I don't</u>

HOUSEWIFE: <u>and</u> how much is this thing here?

SALESMAN: um cheaper them (.) them are two ninety-nine

HOUSEWIFE: oh (.) I don't know

SALESMAN: you can use (.) them like for (.) in well wet and dry as well

HOUSEWIFE: for what?

SALESMAN: wet and dry (.) you can use them for taking condensation off and like putting soap <u>on</u>

HOUSEWIFE: <u>okay</u> I'll buy one of those thank you

Commentary

The housewife basically asks questions for different reasons. First, she asks questions when she needs information: 'it's a what?' and 'for what?' indicate that she hasn't understood something the salesman has said. 'It's a what?' indicates that she hasn't understood his term 'sponge mitts'. 'For what?' means she hasn't understood how they can be used wet and dry and needs an explanation. Obviously, there are questions, too, that ask for simple information about price, such as 'how much is the sponge mitts?'

Some questions seem to stem almost from a desire to draw some conclusions and pull together what information has been given. 'How much are they then?' comes after a declaration that the chamois have been reduced. The tag question, 'they're not very cheap then are they?', goes one stage further. It draws a not very flattering conclusion – that the sponge mitts are not cheap and stresses this with the word 'then'.

In fact, three times in the conversation, tag questions appear after negative evaluation: 'it's a weird assortment of things isn't it?', 'they'll still be six ninety-nine wouldn't they?', and, as already mentioned, 'they're not very cheap then are they?' The tag question appears to be used, therefore, as a device to soften the challenge of a negative statement.

Much of the conversation is concerned with pointing out and explaining what items the salesman has on offer. Because the items are obviously on display to both parties, there is a lot of deitic language such as 'them ones' and 'this'. The hardest part of the transcription to understand is the section 'this is like (.) got all sorts of different bits in (.) if you have an accident'. The vague language, 'all sorts of different bits', isn't clear, though the word 'this' obviously shows the salesman pointing to what, in fact, is an emergency medical kit.

It could be argued that 'then' mentioned previously acts as an discourse marker, showing a conclusion or summary. There is a series of other discourse markers, such as 'anyway', 'well', 'right' and 'and then'. 'Well', 'and then' and 'right' are used to separate out the individual items that the salesman has on offer, in, for example, the utterance 'well there's men's and then there's ladies' hankies as well right we got super scissors . . .'. After talking about the medical kit, 'anyway' marks a return from this discussion to the proper business of the conversation which is to introduce and sell the items in his bag.

The end of the transaction is obvious. The housewife's speech has already overlapped the salesman's several times as she increasingly seems to be impatient to bring the conversation to its end. The final utterance starts with an 'okay' which signals her decision, 'I'll buy one of these'.

'Thank you' is a final, polite way of closing the deal.

Many grammatical features show that the salesman is not just using colloquial language, but is also speaking in dialect. 'Them', for example, appears in 'them ones', and 'them are two ninety-nine', instead of the more standard 'those'. The term of address 'love' also reflects a common way of addressing strangers in that area.

Summary

- ◎ A service encounter means a transaction takes place.
- ◎ Ellipsis and deictic language are usually present.
- ◎ Discourse markers organise the structure.

Learning encounters

We have already looked briefly at this particular conversation genre in Unit three on structure. The main characteristics for this genre are:

- ◎ The teacher takes most turns.
- ◎ The teacher's turns are longer than the students'.
- ◎ The structure is based on adjacency triplets or exchanges (initiation, response and feedback).
- ◎ Discourse markers are used by the teacher to signpost the structure of the conversation.
- ◎ The teacher reformulates, summarises and evaluates what the students say.
- ◎ The students' answers are usually short and elliptical.
- ◎ The teacher uses 'known answer' or 'display' questions (i.e. questions to which they already know the answer).

Activity

Two transcriptions follow: one of a politics lesson, one of a philosophy lesson. Both lessons took place in two separate A-level classes in a sixth form college. The classes are mixed, but the gender of the student has not been indicated in the first transcription. The teacher in the politics lesson is female and in her early forties. The teacher in the second transcription is male, in his early thirties. Examine the two transcriptions for the features of the genre and use your answers to compare and contrast the way the two lessons work.

Text: The politics lesson

TEACHER: right (.) so impact on the UK then (.) this is your essay then (.) and you are doing government and politics A-level (2) so if you had to do a rough draft of the essay and that's all we're going to do today (.) like bullet points (.) what (1) parts of British politics do you feel you would need paragraph after paragraph on? c'mon (.) the order is irrelevant.

STUDENT 1:   parliament

TEACHER: yes (.) parliament good (.) impact on parliament yes very good but even before that the very big one (4) the one we spent the last half term doing

STUDENT 2:   constitution

TEACHER: good (.) constitution good 'cos that would then fit in with the practical operation of constitutions which is parliament (2) and also in particular which underpinning principle of constitution? (1)

STUDENT 3:   parliamentary <u>sov</u>

TEACHER: <u>parliamentary</u> sovereignty (.) good (.) right we're going to be up and running (.) and that is obviously the sort of thing people worry about most (.) that sort of theoretically constitutional background and the difference between Europe and Britain good (3) again, thinking about the second and third principles of the constitution because Europe to some extent has taken to some extent our sovereignty what would we look at? (.) c'mon you got sovereignty of parliament, what's the other?

STUDENT 4:   judiciary

TEACHER: judiciary (.) so you'd have to look at the legal system (.) and if you like the judiciary and obviously people who are going to go on and do law (.) as most of you are thinking of doing (.) that's gonna be (.) that's gonna turn up in an interview next year

Text: The philosophy lesson

TEACHER: Gemma do you think that people can be born leaders?

GEMMA: yeah

TEACHER: go on

GEMMA: 'cause I think you've either got it chemically in you (.) and you've (.) you've got the like confidence and (.) the ability to say what you think and (.) be able to tell that to other people (.) or you haven't

TEACHER: mmmmmmm

GEMMA: some people just (.) really can't do it like they don't (.) have it (.) don't have like the <u>sense</u>

TEACHER: <u>mmmmmmm</u>

GEMMA: <u>to</u> be able to delegate and put across to other people

TEACHER: mmmm (.) okay (.) so what about the sort of precept if somebody said well if you go on a an assertiveness training course (.) that'd be timid or something like that (.) you'd say you're really wasting your time if you were of a certain type (.) all of that kind of stuff is superfluous (.) it won't do you any good (.) so if (.) if you were born a certain (.) certain leader type and that's (.) you can (.) you can develop it one way or the other but a lot of people just fall in-between

MATTHEW: I don't think that's true sir (.) you've got (.) correct me if I'm wrong here but (2) but the qualities of leadership are actually being sort of assertive and

GEMMA: <u>you don't</u> have to be necessarily be assertive to be a good leader

TEACHER: <u>no</u>

GEMMA: it's (.) it's the way (.) the way that you handle things and the way that you process things

MATTHEW: yeah (.) and vice versa someone can be taught to be assertive and it just won't do them any good

Activity

The following conversation took place between a grandmother and a 3-year-old grandchild in the grandchild's home The girl was sitting talking to her grandmother while together they coloured in a colouring book. How many language features similar to those in a classroom conversation can you find?

Text: Colouring in

LAUREN: (*laugh*) I'm cunnin mine in (.) cull dat rabbit in (3) I'm cullin mine in look see? (4) (*inaudible*)

NAN: what are you colourin?

LAUREN: erm (.) a girl (.) a girl (.) a boy (.) some ducks (.) a doggy (.) a (.) look (.) them trees

NAN: what are they?

LAUREN: birds

NAN: ohh (5) (*sigh*) what colour are rabbits?

LAUREN: erm green

NAN: green rabbits?

LAUREN: yeah

NAN: I've never seen a green rabbit (.) I think I'll do my rabbit brown

LAUREN: ha (.) I haven't got brown (.) they're not brown

NAN: I think they are (7)

LAUREN: I've got brown

NAN: how many rabbits have I got?

LAUREN: one, two (.) one, two

NAN: how many can you count up to?

LAUREN: one (.) one (.) one two three four five six seben aight nine ten (.) eleven zwellf triten fourtine fiftin sebentin eight twenty

NAN: ah seventeen (.) eighteen (.) nineteen (.) twenty

LAUREN: I done it

NAN: that's right that's very good

Commentary

The conversation appears similar to that in the classroom because one person, in this case Nan, directs it, introducing most of the topics through the use of mainly known answer questions. The structure of the conversation is, therefore, very dependent on adjacency pairs of question and answer, for example:

NAN: what are you colourin?
LAUREN: erm (.) a girl (.) a girl (.) a boy, etc.

An adjacency triplet also occurs:

NAN: what colour are rabbits?
LAUREN: erm green
NAN: green rabbits?

The feedback of 'green rabbits?' is formulated as a question to evaluate Lauren's previous response of green and indirectly to challenge it. Nan also reformulates Lauren's response, when she repeats Lauren's counting, saying 'ah seventeen (.) eighteen (.) nineteen (.) twenty', and, again, indirectly shows Lauren what the correct pronunciation is. Nan's final evaluation, 'that's right, that's very good', encourages Lauren and confirms that she is right to celebrate her achievement.

Nan is obviously guiding Lauren through the structure and content of the conversation but she is also teaching Lauren about the interactive nature of conversation through her use of politeness. She does show what she really thinks about the colour of rabbits when she says 'I've never seen a green rabbit (.) I think I'll do my rabbit brown', but she never directly says that Lauren is wrong. She shows by example rather than by a direct challenge to Lauren's ideas and viewpoint. Nan's repetition of Lauren's final numbers is typical of conversation conducted between carers and young children. The carers respond to content more than correctness, but illustrate correctness through repetition or reformulation in an unchallenging, indirect way that provides an example that the child can copy and learn from.

Summary

◎   As with all written texts, spoken language produces a variety of conversational genres.

◎   Some elements of a genre are obligatory, some optional.

◎   The language features of a genre reflect the purpose and context of that genre.

Extension

Only some examples of common conversational genre have been discussed in this chapter. There are several, for example, created by the media.

1   Find a sports event covered by both TV and radio. Transcribe the same few minutes of action from both the TV and radio commentaries. Compare and contrast the language features in both transcriptions to investigate which features are obligatory to the genre and which are individual to the different media.

2   Unit four has already used language taken from *Trisha*'s chat show. Compare the data from *Trisha*'s chat show with similar data from another TV chat show.

3   Record and transcribe an extract from two radio phone-in programmes on different radio stations. What features have they in common that establish their particular genre and what features reflect the different purpose and audience of the two programmes?

Spoken language in written texts

So far in this book, we have explained how the features of spoken language and conversation operate in the real world. In this unit, we explore how this knowledge has been applied by writers and has become part of the construction of written texts.

Poetry

It was traditionally accepted that poetic language deviated from the norms and conventions of everyday usage. In contrast to this, however, the late twentieth century has seen the strong influence of spoken language on poetry. There are many reasons for this:

◎ The desire to write about ordinary, everyday aspects of life led to the usage of colloquial language that suited the subject matter.

◎ Poets wanted to demystify poetry so that it was accessible to all readers.

◎ Some Afro-Caribbean poets, for example, wanted to move away from a standard language which was seen as aggressive.

◎ Spoken language was used in poetry to create and develop character. Sometimes, the writer used the whole poem to explore writing in someone else's voice.

◎ The use of language not normally expected in poetry was sometimes a deliberate desire to shock or, conversely, a desire to make shocking taboo language more acceptable.

Activity

The following poem, written in 1999, is by Steven Waling. Read the poem and answer the following questions:

1 What connotations does the title have?
2 What features of spoken language can you spot? What effect do they have on the reader?
3 What topics does the narrator address in the poem?
4 What is the importance of the final verse?

Text: **What She Said**

Didn't have any pain. More an ache
across my shoulders, down my left arm.
Dad wanted me so I joined the Rechabites.*
Mind, I didn't fancy life without a drink.

Knew what it was. I'd read all about it,
and seen it. *True posterior infarct*, that's
what they wrote. I met Eunice through
them: we used to swap each other's clothes.

You could have wrung me out like a dishcloth.
Never knew I'd so much sweat. Anyway, it
weren't as if I ever drank much. Still, I once
won a poetry book, the sort I liked that rhymed.

I always have to be different. Your dad
was in agony, not me: nothing. Well anyway,
now Eunice walks sideways downstairs, fat,
can hardly get out the door. I don't like salad,

and she does. I've got bruises all up my legs,
one right up here. Don't know what from.
Did I tell you I fainted once on the coach
from Blackpool? They said I couldn't even

have a medicinal rum. Just one of those things,
it happens. It's not as if I ever ate, I mean,
you're just going along and … not even a nip.
So anyway, I decided to leave the Rechabites.

* A teetotal Christian group

Commentary

The title indicates immediately that the poem is reporting back on a conversation heard previously.

The following features of conversation are obvious:

◎ Simple, everyday vocabulary, such as 'dishcloth', 'stairs', 'sweat' and 'salad'.

◎ Clichés such as 'just one of those things', and 'you could have wrung me out like a dishcloth'.

◎ Discourse markers such as 'anyway', and 'well anyway', which indicate a return to the main topic after a digression, and 'so anyway', which indicates a final summary statement.

◎ A question to introduce a new topic, 'Did I tell you I fainted once on the coach from Blackpool?'

◎ Personal attitude and evaluation often evident in spoken narratives, 'I didn't fancy life without a drink'.

◎ Dialect grammar, 'It weren't as if I ever drank much'.

All the spoken features mean that the poem takes on the immediacy and directness of a spoken voice. The detail of the dialect, for example, creates a distinctive character for the voice that the reader can identify with. Instead of the detachment and distance of reported language, it is as if we are present as the words are spoken. What the woman says, therefore, becomes very real and our listening becomes almost part of the context for the conversation. We are providing an audience for the speaker, who is using conversation to explore her own personal feelings.

Two topics compete throughout the poem. Discussion of the speaker's recent heart attack is interwoven with her recollections of joining and then finally leaving the Rechabites, a society that believed in complete abstinence from alcohol. Eunice, the speaker's old friend, also gets mentioned. The frequent switching of topics and apparent lack of overall purpose to the conversation reflect the structure of conversation often found between speakers who know each other well.

All the topics come together in the final verse. Familiar with Grice's most important maxim, be relevant, the reader attempts to work out the connection between the Rechabites' refusal to allow even a medicinal rum and the suddenness of her heart attack, 'You're just going along and . . .'. The heart attack seems to have jogged the speaker's memory of a trip to Blackpool when she fainted unexpectedly. Her decision to leave the Rechabites indicates an irritation with a society whose method of prolonging life suddenly seemed ridiculously rigid when it wouldn't even allow the speaker alcohol to help her recover from her faint. The reader has already experienced the irony that it is the salad-loving Eunice who is fat. The final verse seems, therefore, to continue the speaker's exploration of the illogical nature of illness and death. The definite rejection of the Rechabites and their attempts to control these inexplicable forces appear to signal the woman's acceptance of her fate and the futility of torturing herself with questioning why the heart attack happened and how she could have prevented it. As she says, 'it's just one of those things, it happens'.

Novels

Even in a spoken narrative, people frequently report back and use voices to convey what other people have said in order to make their narrative more real and vivid. Some novelists give their narrator a clear, distinctive voice, with which they tell the whole story. In most novels, writers use dialogue for a variety of purposes:

- to present and develop character;
- to further the plot;
- to allow characters to explore themes and ideas of the novel;
- to create atmosphere;
- to present different points of view.

The speech of any individual is unique. Each individual has been influenced by their gender, age, occupation, social class, temperament and regional dialect, so that they create their own **idiolect** or personal style of speaking. This is often caught by a novelist who will use dialogue to mark out the individuality of their character. Studies of accent and dialect have also revealed how, as individuals, we act as representatives of different groups in society. Dialect can operate, therefore, to show a character's particular region, social occupation, class or even, to some extent, gender.

Because of society's in-built attitude to different non-standard accents and dialects, both can also be used for the following:

- to show integrity in a character;
- to provide comedy;
- to show simplicity or lack of education;
- to show intimacy.

Activity

The following conversation is taken from *Sense and Sensibility* by Jane Austen. Previously, Elinor has fallen in love with Edward. Lucy, suspicious of Elinor's feelings, warns Elinor off, by revealing her own relationship with Edward. Read the extract and answer the following questions:

1　How does Jane Austen capture the prosodic features and body language of conversation? What effect does this have on the reader?

2　How does Jane Austen provide different spoken language for her two speakers? What do the differences show about the two characters?

3　What advantage is there in using dialogue rather than any other form of narration?

Text: *Sense and Sensibility*

'Good heavens!' cried Elinor, 'what do you mean? Are you acquainted with Mr Robert Ferrars? Can you be?' And she did not feel much delighted with the idea of such a sister-in-law.

'No,' replied Lucy, 'not with Mr *Robert* Ferrars – I never saw him in my life; but,' fixing her eyes upon Elinor, 'with his elder brother.'

What felt Elinor at that moment? Astonishment, that would have been as painful as it was strong had not an immediate disbelief of the assertion attended it. She turned towards Lucy in silent amazement, unable to divine the reason or object of such a declaration; and though her complexion varied, she stood firm in incredulity, and felt in no danger of an hysterical fit or a swoon.

'You may well be surprised,' continued Lucy; 'for, to be sure, you could have had no idea of it before; for I dare say he never dropped the smallest hint of it to you or any of your family; because it was always meant to be a great secret, and I am sure has been faithfully kept so by me to this hour. Not a soul of all my relations know of it but Anne, and I never should have mentioned it to you, if I had not felt the greatest dependence in the world upon your secrecy; and I really thought my behaviour in asking so many questions about Mrs Ferrars must seem so odd that it ought to be explained. And I do not think Mr Ferrars can be displeased when he knows I have trusted you, because I know he has the highest opinion in the world of all your family, and looks upon yourself and the other Miss Dashwoods quite as his own sisters.' – She paused.

Elinor for a few moments remained silent. Her astonishment at what she heard was at first too great for words; but at length forcing herself to speak, and to speak cautiously, she said with a calmness of manner which tolerably well concealed her surprise and solicitude – 'May I ask if your engagement is of long standing?'

'We have been engaged these four years.'

'Four years!'

'Yes.'

Elinor, though greatly shocked, still felt unable to believe it.

'I did not know,' said she, 'that you were even acquainted till the other day.'

'Our acquaintance, however, is of many years' date. He was under my uncle's care, you know, a considerable while.'

'Your uncle!'

'Yes, Mr Pratt. Did you never hear him talk of Mr Pratt?'

'I think I have,' replied Elinor, with an exertion of spirits which increased with her increase of emotion.

'He was four years with my uncle, who lives at Longstaple, near Plymouth. It was there our acquaintance begun, for my sister and me was often staying with my uncle, and it was there our engagement was formed, though not till a year after he had quitted as a pupil; but he was almost always with us afterwards. I was very unwilling to enter into it, as you may imagine, without the knowledge and approbation of his mother; but I was too young and loved him too well to be so prudent as I ought to have been. – Though you do not know him so well as me, Miss Dashwood, you must have seen enough of him to be sensible he is very capable of making a woman sincerely attached to him.'

'Certainly,' answered Elinor, without knowing what she said.

Commentary

The rising intonation of Elinor's voice as she feels surprise is caught simply in the word 'cried'. In contrast, later in the extract, we are told she spoke with 'a calmness of manner'. Lucy's body language is clearly described twice, 'She looked down as she said this, amiably bashful, with only one side glance at her companion to observe its effect on her', and later we are told she spoke, 'fixing her eyes upon Elinor'. The body language is in complete contrast to the apparent simple sincerity of her disclosure – the eyes and side glance indicating almost a challenge as she checks the effect her words are having on Elinor.

Even the length of utterances shows a clear difference between the two characters. Lucy's verbosity means her utterances are clearly longer than Elinor's. Jane Austen starts Lucy's sentence with 'And' in 'And I do not think Mr Ferrars can be displeased', the typical conjunction used in spoken language emphasising the rapidity of her speech. The sentences contain many unnecessary fillers, such as 'for to be sure' and 'for I dare say', and the impression given is of a verbose, rapid speaker. Lucy uses the intensifiers or hyperbole of exaggerated, dramatic language in expressions such as 'the smallest hint', 'the greatest dependence', 'the highest opinion', and 'I was too young and loved him too well'. She is given non-standard dialect to speak, saying, 'My sister and me was often staying with my uncle'.

Elinor, in contrast, gives clear and direct replies. We are told she does not reveal her feelings, but 'concealed her surprise and solicitude', and her language merely shows politeness in her request, 'May I ask if your engagement is of long standing?' She also does not show any signs of non-standard grammar or vocabulary.

The differences in language show the differences between the two characters. Lucy appears uneducated, superficial and insincere. Elinor, in contrast, seems thoughtful, reserved and of a superior social status.

We have been given information about the plot and characters here. By allowing the characters to present themselves in dialogue rather than the narrator passing on the information, the reader becomes more involved in the novel, interpreting the characters as they would real people overheard in conversation. The variety in language used in the voices adds depth and variety to the language of the novel and its similarity to spoken language gives the reader something to identify with and relate to. The whole scene becomes vivid and real.

Drama

The whole of a play is obviously based on action and dialogue. The dialogue is not the same as that produced in real life. Overlaps, where two speakers talk simultaneously, are usually not present, though Caryl Churchill in *Top Girls* has experimented with dialogue that does have characters talking at the same time. The typical non-fluency features produced either to self-correct or due to the spontaneity of spoken language are greatly reduced in number. The utterances tend to be longer than those in normal conversation and more grammatically correct. There will usually be less ellipsis, less deictic language and the speakers spend longer developing and exploring their topics.

As in novels, the vocabulary and grammar given to individual characters will give them an idiolect that strengthens the impression they create on an audience. The way the characters speak will give the audience information about where they come from, in regional and social terms, their level of education, their occupation, interests and even gender and personality.

Because language can only fully be understood when its context and purpose are known, the writer can try to ensure his or her perception of context in the production of a play. This can be done with stage directions which, at times, enable the audience to be aware of the following:

- the setting of the scene;
- the action of the characters;
- the body language of the characters;
- the characters' tone of voice.

Even the punctuation of the text can help here as 'I love you!' means something completely different from 'I love you?' A writer's attempt to be precise with these directions shows the awareness that the individual meanings of words communicate far less than the meaning they create in use. The pragmatics of the language – that is, the speaker meaning in context as opposed to the linguistic surface meaning of an utterance – is what dramatists have to explore in their writing.

Sometimes, for example, conflict between characters in a play seems to rest not on something that has actually been said but more on something that remains unsaid. A dramatist has to work, therefore, on implied as well as literal meaning.

Knowledge, therefore, of how individuals relate to each other in conversation is a prerequisite for good dramatic writing. The use or lack of politeness strategies in dialogue can highlight close relationships or areas of conflict. Many features already discussed can be used to explore relationships in dialogue. Some interesting features to consider may be:

◎   the observance or otherwise of Grice's maxims;
◎   the use of questions;
◎   repetition;
◎   evaluation and reformulation;
◎   refusal to take up a topic;
◎   provisional or conditional language;
◎   silences;
◎   commands;
◎   hedges;
◎   vague language.

As listeners in a conversation help to construct its meaning, so too do the audience of a play. As the actors work to display meaning, the audience works to interpret the meaning, constructing it from their own experience and knowledge of language in context.

Because drama is artificially constructed by a writer, however, the dialogue created can be used to challenge the audience. If, for example, characters do not react or talk in a way that the audience would have predicted, this challenges the audience's preconceived ideas and provides new ideas for debate. This can be where drama leads the audience beyond the boundaries of normal conversation.

Activity

The following is an extract from *Othello* by William Shakespeare. It is taken from Act 3, Scene 3 and is where Iago, Othello's ensign, is tempting him to believe that Othello's wife, Desdemona, has been unfaithful with Cassio. Desdemona has just left the stage and Othello starts the extract by exploring his feelings for her. Read the extract and answer the following questions:

1   What is implied in this conversation but not said?
2   How is it implied?
3   How does Shakespeare show the body language he expects Iago to use and why is this important?
4   What relationship exists between the two speakers?

Text: *Othello*

OTHELLO: Excellent wretch! Perdition catch my soul
   But I do love thee; and when I love thee not,
   Chaos is come again.
IAGO: My noble lord –
OTHELLO: What dost thou say, Iago?
IAGO: Did Michael Cassio,
   When you wooed my lady, know of your love?
OTHELLO: He did from first to last. Why dost thou ask?
IAGO: But for a satisfaction of my thought;
   No further harm.
OTHELLO: Why of thy thought, Iago?
IAGO: I did not think he had been acquainted with her.
OTHELLO: O yes, and went between us very oft.
IAGO: Indeed?
OTHELLO: Indeed? Ay, indeed. Discern'st though aught in that?
   Is he not honest?
IAGO: Honest, my lord?
OTHELLO: Honest? Ay honest.
IAGO: My lord, for aught I know.
OTHELLO: What dost thou think?
IAGO: Think, my lord
OTHELLO: Think, my lord! By heaven, he echoes me,
   As if there were some monster in his thought
   Too hideous to be shown. Thou dost mean something.
   I heard thee say even now thou lik'st not that,
   When Cassio left my wife. What didst not like?
   And when I told thee he was of my counsel
   In my whole course of wooing, thou cried'st 'Indeed?'
   And didst contract and purse thy brow together,
   As if thou then hadst shut up in thy brain
   Some horrible conceit. If thou dost love me,
   Show me thy thought.
IAGO: My lord, you know I love you.

Commentary

Iago implies he knows something about Cassio that he does not want to reveal. The implication is also that what he knows concerns Cassio's relationship with Othello's wife, Desdemona. That he doesn't want to reveal what he knows also implies that it is something negative.

First, Iago introduces the topic with his question, 'Did Michael Cassio,/ When you wooed my lady, know of your love?' His refusal then to answer Othello's questions properly, 'Why dost thou ask?', 'Why of thy thought, Iago?' and 'Discern'st thou aught in that?', is contrary to expected behaviour in conversation. Again, the repetition in the following exchanges implies more than it actually says.

> OTHELLO: Is he not honest?
> IAGO: Honest, my lord?
> OTHELLO: Honest? Ay honest.
>
> OTHELLO: What dost thou think?
> IAGO: Think my lord?
> OTHELLO: Think, my lord!

Iago repeats what Othello says almost in the way that a parent can repeat a child's utterance in order to question what they have said and to get them to develop the topic further. By answering Othello's questions with his own questions, Iago has effectively refused to take up Othello's topics. Iago's final response to Othello's question about Cassio's honesty, 'My lord for aught I know', is dismissive. Even at the end of the exchange, when Othello orders Iago to 'Show me thy thought', Iago refuses to elaborate on the topic and effectively changes the topic, saying, 'My lord, you know I love you'. Because Othello is aware of Grice's maxim – be relevant – the implication of this change of topic leaves him uncertain and doubtful. If Iago loves him, why can't he answer the question? Iago's unwillingness to take up the topic must be because he is thinking something he knows Othello would not want to hear and, as a friend, he would not want to say.

Iago's responses have obviously been spoken with some emotion as Othello tells us he 'cried'st "Indeed?"' Iago's body language also implies that his reluctance to elaborate is suspicious. Shakespeare gets Othello to describe his body language for us when he says that Iago,

> dids't contract and purse thy brow together,
> As if thou then hadst shut up in thy brain
> Some horrible conceit.

Obviously, the concern Iago has shown on his face has contradicted the apparent lack of interest shown in his replies. His body language is a clear device to illustrate that his words should not be taken at face value.

The extract shows an interesting relationship between the two men. Although Othello has more status than Iago, it appears very much that Iago is directing and leading the conversation. Almost like a teacher introducing a topic and leading the pupils to discuss it, Iago is making Othello guess what's in his mind. Iago's refusal to elaborate leads Othello to say, 'he echoes me,/As if there were some monster in his thought/Too hideous to be shown', and the audience can clearly hear that Othello has been manipulated into thinking exactly what Iago wants him to think.

Summary

◎ Spoken language in literature is a stylised, constructed version of real spoken language.

◎ The features of spoken language used in literature create a variety of voices that develop character.

◎ The use of voices exploits and explores society's attitudes to class, region, occupation and gender.

◎ Features of conversation can be used to show relationships between characters and to explore conflict.

◎ The audience is involved in creating the context for spoken language and in interpreting its meaning.

◎ The use of spoken language can make the texts more informal and demystify them.

◎ An unexpected use of spoken language can challenge an audience to rethink attitudes and preconceived ideas.

Extension

1 Many modern twentieth-century poets have used voices in their poetry; U.A. Fanthorpe, for example, in *The Sheepdog*. Take this poem and look at the language features she has used to create the sheepdog's voice and explain why she has done this.

2 *Trainspotting*, by Irvine Welsh, challenges the accepted practice of writing novels in standard English. Take the opening to this novel and look at the voice created for the narrator. Examine what features of spoken language are present in both the grammar and vocabulary used and discuss what effect this has on the reader.

3   Watch and transcribe an extract from one of your favourite soap operas. How does the language used differ from conversation in real life? How has the writer used features of conversation to show the relationships between the characters?

index of terms

This is a form of combined glossary and index. Listed below are some of the main key terms used in the book, together with brief definitions for purposes of reference. The page references will normally take you to the first use of the term in the book, where it is shown in bold.

adjacency pairs 3

These are the pairs of utterances that commonly occur, such as question–answer, introduction–greeting.

conversational implicature 38

This is the meaning that is conveyed when one of Grice's maxims is deliberately flouted.

deictics 37

Deitics are words which point backwards, forwards and extra textually and which serve to situate a speaker or writer in relation to what is said. In 'I'm going to get some wine from that shop over there', the main deictic words are 'that' and 'there'.

discourse markers 11

These are words such as 'well' and 'right' which are normally used to mark boundaries in conversation between one topic and the next. They can also signpost relationships between utterances.

ellipsis 11

Ellipsis refers to the omission of part of a structure. It is normally used for reasons of economy and, in spoken discourse, can create a sense of informality. For example, in the sentence, 'She went to the party and danced all night', the pronoun 'she' is ellipsed from the second clause. In the dialogue:

> You going to the party?
> Might be

the verb 'are' and the pronoun 'I', respectively, are omitted, with ellipsis here creating a casual and informal tone.

exchange 28

A basic pattern of structuring interaction that often occurs in classroom conversation. It consists of three moves known as initiation, response and follow-up or feedback.

filler 18

Fillers are items which do not carry conventional meaning, but which are inserted, usually in spoken discourse, to allow time to think, to create a pause, and so on.

frame theory 63

This theory argues that past experiences help us to understand conversation. From our past conversations we bring mental frameworks that help us to understand and anticipate what is going to happen next in a conversation. As we talk we pick up cues (or frames) that enable us to recognise the situation and structure our response in an appropriate manner.

Grice's maxims 38

The co-operative principle was formulated by Grice (1975) to explain the assumptions made by people in constructing talk. The speaker should follow four maxims: be brief, be true, be relevant and be clear. The listener should assume the speaker is following these four maxims.

hedges 53

Hedges are words and phrases which soften or weaken the force with which something is said. Examples of hedges are: 'kind of', 'sort of', 'by any chance', 'as it were', 'admittedly'.

idiolect 82

This is the language special or peculiar to an individual. It is sometimes known as a 'personal' dialect.

insertion sequence 28

A sequence of utterances separating an adjacency pair.

A: Do you want a drink?
B: What have you got?
A Everything you can think of including a cup of tea!
B: Well, I'll have tea then

interactional language 25

The language used when people relate to each other – the language used for socialising.

intonation 2

This is the rise and fall in pitch that occurs in spoken language.

pragmatic meaning (see **pragmatics**)

pragmatics 38

What the speaker is doing or intending with the words. The speaker meaning in context as opposed to the linguistic surface meaning of an utterance.

prosodic features 2

These are features of the voice such as speed, volume, intonation and stress.

pseudo-agreement 54

This is used to save face. It occurs when one speaker appears at first to agree with another. In continuing the utterance, however, the speaker expresses a viewpoint that differs from the initial agreement.

A: Do you like classical music?
B: Yes but I prefer listening to jazz.

service encounter 69

This is a transactional conversation where requests made by one person to another are dealt with and answered.

speaker support 18

This in conversation is the feedback given from a listener to a speaker. The purpose of the feedback is to let the speaker know they are being listened to and to encourage the speaker to continue.

speech acts 5

A speech act refers to what is done when something is said (for example, warning, threatening, promising, requesting). 'I declare the meeting open', in this sense does what it says. An 'indirect speech act' has a meaning which is different from its apparent meaning. For example, the question, 'Is that your coat on the floor?' could *indirectly* suggest that the coat should be picked up.

speech event 6

A use of language in a social context in which the speakers normally follow a set of agreed rules and conventions. For example, telling a joke, recounting a story, purchasing stamps in a post office, are all speech events.

tag questions 19

Tags are strings of words which are normally added to a declarative statement and which turn the statement into a question, for example, 'It's cold, isn't it?'

transactional language 25

Language that is used in obtaining goods and services.

utterance indicator (see **discourse marker**)

vague language 11

Written language is usually precise. Vague language, such as 'or something' and 'or whatever', occurs deliberately in spoken language to soften the impact made by the speaker.

voiced pauses 8

Noises made by a speaker such as 'er' or 'um' which give the speaker time to pause and indicate a desire to hold the speaking turn.

references

Austin, J.L. (1962) *How to Do Things with Words* (New York, Oxford University Press)

Beard, A. (2000) *The Language of Politics* (London, Routledge)

Brown, G. and Yule, G. (1983) *Discourse Analysis* (Cambridge, Cambridge University Press)

Brown, P. and Levinson, S.C. (1978) *Politeness: Some Universals in Language Usage* (Cambridge, Cambridge University Press)

Carter, R. and McCarthy, M. (1997) *Exploring Spoken English* (Cambridge, Cambridge University Press)

Coates, J. (1986) *Women, Men and Language* (London, Longman)

Cook, G. (1989) *Discourse* (Oxford, Oxford University Press)

Goddard, A. and Patterson, L. (2000) *Language and Gender* (London, Routledge)

Goffman, E. (1974) *Frame Analysis* (New York, Harper & Row)

Grice, H.P. (1975) 'Logic and conversation', in Cole, P. and Morgan, J. (eds) *Syntax and Semantics*, vol. 3 *Speech Acts* (New York, Academic Press), pp. 41–58

Gumperz, J.J. (1982) *Discourse Strategies* (Cambridge, Cambridge University Press)

Halliday, M.A.K. (1973) *Explorations in the Functions of Language* (London, Arnold)

Labov, W. (1972) 'The transformation of experience in narrative syntax', in Labov, W., *Language in the Inner City* (Philadelphia, University of Philadelphia), pp. 354–96

Lakoff, R. (1973) 'The logic of politeness: minding your p's and q's', papers from the Ninth Regional Meeting, Chicago Linguistics Society, pp. 292–305

Levinson, S. (1983) *Pragmatics* (Cambridge, Cambridge University Press)

McArthur, T. (1992) *Concise Oxford Companion to the English Language* (Oxford, Oxford University Press)

Montgomery, M. (1995) *An Introduction to Language and Society* (London, Routledge)

Sacks, H., Schegloff, E. and Jefferson, G. (1974) 'A simple systematics for the organisation of turn-taking for conversation', *Language*, 50, 4, 696–735

Schiffrin, D. (1987) *Discourse Markers* (Cambridge, Cambridge University Press)

Searle, J. (1969) *Speech Acts: An Essay in the Philosophy of Language* (Cambridge, Cambridge University Press)

Sinclair, J. and Coulthard, R.M. (1975) *Toward an Analysis of Discourse* (Oxford, Oxford University Press)

Stubbs, M. (1983) *Discourse Analysis* (Oxford, Blackwell)

Tannen, D. (1991) *You Just Don't Understand: Women and Men in Conversation* (London, Virago Press)

Ventola, E. (1987) *The Structure of Social Interaction: A Systemic Approach to the Semiotics of Service Encounters* (London, Frances Pinter)